Endorsements for *Free to Dream*

So often fear is the monster lingering in the space between you and your dreams, keeping you from living in the fullness of your God-given destiny. But the truth is, the Lord has intended for His perfect love to cast out fear and for you to live in the fullness of what He paid for on the cross. In *Free to Dream*, Heather shares a vital message for every believer's journey into true freedom. In the pages of this book, you will be inspired by Heather's journey of overcoming fear to quit walking on eggshells, leave the land of familiarity, and be empowered to take the courageous step into your destiny.

KRIS VALLOTTON
Leader, Bethel Church, Redding, CA
Co-Founder of Bethel School of Supernatural Ministry
Author of twelve books including, *Uprising: The Epic Battle for the Most Fatherless Generation in History* and *Spiritual Intelligence*.

Heather has been a family friend for a number of years. Both of us admire her courage, faith, and tenacity to pursue her dreams. In her book *Free to Dream*, Heather shares stories that will inspire you, provoke you to dream, and challenge you to face your fears. We have witnessed her pursuing her dreams and know that through this must-read you, too, can gain the courage to pursue yours.

PEDRO AND SUZETTE ADAO
Founders Of 100X the #1 Training Program and Community for Kingdom Entrepreneurs

At one time or another, I believe we have all felt "stuck." Perhaps it was a relationship, a job, or even a weight-loss journey. When we feel stuck, it limits our ability to dream and risk. I believe that Heather's new book *Free to Dream* will get you "unstuck" and launch you into a journey of vision and possibility. God has a great plan for you, and sometimes we need a good book and a friend to help us realize that. Heather is a true pioneer and advocate for women to look beautiful, live boldly, and celebrate one another. I honor her, and I am proud to be her friend. This book will be a great catalyst for your life, and I'm thrilled to watch the world explode with passion-filled purposeful women!

JESSI GREEN
Revivalist. Director of Saturate Global
Author of *Wildfires*

In the more than a decade that I have known Heather, she has proven herself one who stares down fear and chases dreams with a tenacity and passion that is inspiring. Some people let fear or pain stop them from dreaming, others only dream, but Heather is one who turns her dreams into reality. I am convinced that her story and insights form a credible pathway for guiding you to the promised land of your heart dream.

DAN (DANO) MCCOLLAM
Co-Founder of Prophetic Company and Bethel School of the Prophets, Author of Love and Prophecy, Bending Time, and more

Free to Dream is so much more than a book of permission; it is a guidebook leading the reader from discovering their authentic identity, embracing it, and then activating it so that their dreams become realities. Heather's vulnerability in sharing her own journey and addressing the issues that hold us prisoner to our wishes offers courage to fellow travelers and opens windows of potential.

DAVID CRONE
Founder of The Mission Vacaville, Author of Decisions That Define Us and The Power of Your Life Message

It has been my joy to know Heather and her husband Keith for 20 years. Heather has even gone to minister in the garbage dumps with my wife Winnie and me. Over the years, I've watched her develop into a powerful and free worshipper with a huge heart for the Lord. I love Heather's joyful, childlike pursuit of her God-given dreams; for she knows Christ is faithful to lead, guide, provide for, and strengthen her every step of the way.

In Heather's book, Free to Dream, she shares her journey over the last years to step into all that God has for her. As you read it, you will be encouraged to let go of fear once and for all and step into your own dreams, pursuing God's best for you.

I highly recommend Heather and her new book; way to go, Heather!

GEORGIAN BANOV
President and Co-Founder of Global Celebration and GCSSM Online School; author of Joy! God's Secret Weapon for Every Believer

Free to Dream is a powerful invitation into more with God. Heather's honest, real, and life-changing stories carry an impartation of hope for you to step into a new way with Jesus. As Heather says in the book, "You're always one decision away from a totally different life." Heather gives tangible examples of how she has seen this firsthand in her own walk with the Lord and links arms with you to walk into that same freedom and breakthrough. Just beautiful.

ELISE TARANGO
Co-Founder of Prophetic Heart Healing in San Diego, CA

Heather takes you on a liberating journey of discovery and freedom in *Free to Dream*. Through her inspiring personal stories of life and faith, you will find yourself identifying with her journey and the life lessons God has taught her along the way. Heather writes with a beautiful authenticity and vulnerability that meets you right where you are in life. And the activations and declarations Heather shares at the end of each chapter will not only help you discover the dreams that reside deep within you, but you will discover how to awaken your dreams so that you might live them!

DENA MCCLURE
Kingdom trainer and equipper

Free to Dream is a must read. Heather has done an amazing job of revealing transparent stories that will bless and amaze those who read this book. Heather is a special woman who God has raised up for such a time as this. Heather and Keith are a couple of my spiritual kids that, as a Kingdom Father, I am deeply proud of, and I know you will receive a special blessing and anointing as you read this book. It is truly like the stones Jacob was instructed to build at his well in the desert to remind the next generation of what the Lord did because God is good. I pray and prophesy to whoever reads this book that you will receive a blessing. I'm honored to know and walk with Heather.

WENDELL MCGOWAN
Prophetic Voice, Las Vegas, NV

I love this book! Heather's vulnerability and lessons learned are essential to breaking the fear barriers with practical applications to get you there. I appreciated the vital, thought-provoking questions many of us never think to ask ourselves. She gives insightful wisdom, both biblical and from her own experiences, on why identity, purpose, and timing are critical steps into your calling. I value strategic books like this that move me into my Kingdom purpose. So, if you're over fear holding you back, you're ready to dream again, and want to actually live it out, start reading and get ready for a breakthrough.

CATHY GREER
Founder, Kingdom Women International & Mission Support Network

I have known Heather Ferrante for a long time and have been a first-hand witness in Heather's life to the unfolding of the lessons in many of the chapters in *Free To Dream*. Heather is authentic and as pure a human as I've ever known. Her journey is worth paying attention to, for in it you will find pathways to your own spiritual growth and freedom, to the release of your own dreams, and to enjoyment of life on planet earth.

REGINA MCCOLLAM
Author of *Intertwined: Strength to Stand*

I've been blessed to be part of Heather's journey for over 25 years. I have seen, firsthand, Heather pressing through fears and doubts to pursue all that God has for her and her family. In these pages, you will find authenticity, truth, vulnerability, and hope. Heather's story is one of breakthrough, not only for herself, but for us as well. This book is about transformation, and I couldn't be more proud of my friend. For those who need freedom, breakthrough, and courage to pursue your dreams, this book is for you.

TARA MCCOY
Ordained minister, educator, and friend

Heather Ferrante is one of the most genuine women of God I have had the privilege of knowing and calling as one of my best friends for over 25 years. Heather lives to see Jesus glorified in all that she does, from being a wife, a mother, and doing hair, to setting "boots" on the ground in the nations. I have watched her journey through the years, seeing the tears, hearing her heart and the relentless wrestlings with the Lord for breakthrough, all while learning to trust Jesus in the process and punching fear in the face. Heather is an overcomer of fear; she has dared to step out and take risks with Jesus in pursuit of her dreams, and the outcome speaks for itself in the pages of this book *Free to Dream*. The book you are holding is a powerful tool to unlock great breakthrough in your life, take you into a deeper love relationship with Jesus, and teaching you how and giving you permission to dream. Just as I was moved and challenged while reading the manuscript, I, too, believe readers will be moved in the depths of their hearts to lean into greater intimacy in pursuit of the more of God, dare to punch fear in the face, dream bigger, step out, and take risks while learning to trust God in the process. Doing the Activations at the end of the chapters and applying the tools in this book will transform you into the lioness you were created to be! Enjoy the journey!

MARY STREET
Co-Founder of Roaring Hope International, Founder of House of Hope Girls Home in Tanzania East Africa, missionary, revivalist

A Masterpiece has many tones, hues, and dimension – created beautifully to cause you to pause, and so it is with this written work. *Free to Dream* is courageously told, called to action and layered with hope.

MONICA SAYAD
Global Leader with World Forum Foundation, Director of the Early Learning Program for The Round Valley Indian Tribes, wife, mother, minister of the Gospel

"Our truest life is when we are in dreams awake." —Henry Thoreau

If you are ready to live your life fully alive and with purposeful intentionality, then Heather's book is a must read! *Free to Dream*, will inspire you to do whatever it takes to overcome fear and step into your YES with God. We are living in a time like none other, and there are destinies and purposes we all have to unlock and step into for Jesus to be known on the earth and for His Glory to be revealed. Heather's book will inspire you to say yes to your dreams and not only say yes, but take action! Her journey of believing God and what He fashioned and created her to walk in completely resonated with my heart and it will speak to yours as well. As women, we can struggle with comparing ourselves to one another, which only keeps us from running our race. Heather's book is a testimony which carries the spirit of prophecy for God to do it again for you.

As you read each chapter, you'll find yourself on a journey of overcoming fear and distractions which have kept you from moving forward with purpose. Heather also includes powerful activations and declarations at the end of each chapter that awaken the dreamer in you. I'm so honored to know Heather, read her journey, and see God move through this book, inspiring a generation of women to step into their dreams and live fully alive!

JOANNE JOHNSON
Founder of Kingdom Women International, Founder of Give4

Free to Dream

© 2022 by Heather Ferrante

ISBN: 9798359003261

FREE TO

Dream

Let Go of Fear and
Step Into Your New Day

HEATHER FERRANTE

Dedication

DEDICATE THIS BOOK TO MY FAMILY. I wouldn't be who I am today without the impact you have all had on my life.

To my husband Keith, you are the love of my life and my best friend. Thank you for being my biggest support and for encouraging me to pursue the dreams of my heart. I love us and the life we have created together. I look forward to many more adventures with you.

To my children, Maci and Micah. I love you both so much and am honored to be your mom. Watching you grow in your personal relationship with the Lord and discover your own dreams is my greatest joy. I pray that the breakthroughs your dad and I have received will truly become the launching pad for the two of you to soar. Always remember that no dream is too big for you if it is in your heart. If you can dream it, you can do it. With God all things are possible.

To my parents, Mike and Donna Tolentino. Dad, as I was finishing this book, you went to Heaven to be with Jesus. I'm so grateful I got to be with you during your last days here on earth. Thank you for all the life lessons you taught me. Our journey together taught me how to love on a deeper level, and for that I will forever be grateful. You are now FREE and experiencing life in the presence of God. I'm honored to have been your daughter. I love you. Mom, your strength and faithfulness is truly inspiring. Thank you for loving our family well, especially Dad. Thank you for raising me with a godly foundation. You taught me to love God with my whole heart and have modeled unconditional love well. I love you and am so thankful you are my mom.

To Pops and Muthie, thank you for being you. Your love and prayers have carried our family through the years and continue to do so. Thank you for being a listening ear and great encouragers. I love you.

To the rest of my family, I love you all very much and pray God's richest blessings on each and every one of you. Thank you for who you are to me.

Chapters

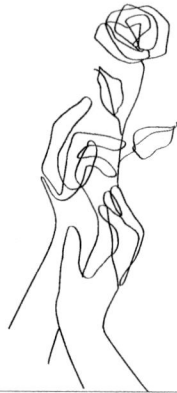

I'M SO THANKFUL GOD GAVE

ME SUCH A WONDERFUL GIFT

IN MY WIFE. I AM SO PROUD

OF HER AND AM SO HAPPY TO

INTRODUCE HER TO YOU.

99

Foreword

BY KEITH FERRANTE

TWENTY-SIX YEARS AGO, IN THE FALL, I met Heather Tolentino. She was not yet Heather Ferrante. That would happen nearly a year later, on October 4, 1997. A friend and I were at Bible college together talking about a new girl who had come to school that year. He and I both had our eye on her. He was interested in her because he heard she had Filipino roots. He was fully Filipino. I, on the other hand, was interested in this gal because from the moment I saw her, I said *that is the lady for me*. Maybe it was how pretty she was, her kind smile, her sweetness that I could perceive from a distance. But whatever it was, I was hooked.

What were we to do about the fact that both of us liked the same girl? Being mature men of God, we prayed. No, not really, LOL...we tossed a coin. Tails she's yours; heads she's mine. So funny! But the coin toss didn't turn out in my favor. I lost. It was tails, and so he won.

But it wasn't over for us. Unbeknownst to me, one of Heather's friends had overheard us talking about the coin toss.

Once a year, our Bible college would host a special date night called Spinster Spree. It was a night where all of the girls were supposed to ask a guy out. Heather's girlfriends were going with my friends, and knowing that I had tossed a coin for her, Heather had the courage to ask me out.

She didn't ask me out through normal means, however. She sent me on a treasure hunt where every clue brought me closer to finding out who was asking me out on that special date. I followed the clues for a while, then finally I went to get into my car and there on my windshield was the last clue. It said this: "Heads, not tails."

I didn't know who was going to ask me out before, but when I saw that last clue, I excitedly knew it was Heather. I hadn't even officially met her at that point. But that was the kind of girl she was even back then – creative, bold, beautiful, pure, and a great example in God.

You see, Heather had grown up in an incredibly challenging environment. I mean truthfully, we all have disfunctions in our family at some level, so this isn't a knock on her family. But it is part of her journey and testimony. Even though she had experienced trauma growing up, she was raised by her mom to go to church. Heather fell in love with Jesus at a young age. Her church environment became a place of safety for her. She was pure and saved her virginity for whoever she was going to marry. She was a rare, beautiful flower. Her name Heather actually means flower from the highlands.

Without her parents knowing, she put herself through counseling and paid for it with her own money while attending college. She learned how to truly forgive, and God healed her heart.

There were still other journeys she had to go on to gain a deeper level of freedom and authority over the trauma and fear she grew up in. But she chose to lean into those journeys later. You will read about some of them in this book.

Growing up, Heather spent time going to Holy Spirit meetings where she received the Holy Spirit, joy, tongues, and more freedom. Even during Bible college she went to a revival that had broken out in Pensacola,

Florida, called the Brownsville Revival. She and three of her girlfriends drove the 12 hours it took to get to the revival hotspot on a weekend during the school year. She got so wrecked in God that she came back to the school laughing in the Holy Spirit with her friends for days. I would see her laughing and then dancing in worship in our chapel services. That was not a normal expression at all for our Bible college, but Heather didn't care. She was always more interested in encountering God than pleasing man.

Not long after those journeys, we met. She did the treasure hunt with the clues for me, and eventually, like I said, I discovered she had invited me on a date with my friends. Now, she didn't really like me yet, but she told me later she thought I had a nice smile. I finally got to officially meet her in a singing group we were a part of together. We said hi, and I told her I got her invitation to the date. She asked me what my answer was. I, being a bit of a romantic, said, "To the ends of the earth."

And that is exactly what happened...

A year later, we were married, and within a couple years were traveling to multiple nations together. As I write this Foreword, we will be celebrating our 25th anniversary within a week. Folks, she's the real deal.

Marrying me sent her on another journey of freedom. I wasn't super healthy in my relational values back then. I was passionate for Jesus and knew I would be in some type of vocational ministry after Bible college, but I had a lot of beliefs from a skewed view of Scripture concerning husband and wife, submission, authority, etc. Those views needed an upgrade.

Some of Heather's friends knew I wasn't perfect in those areas and were concerned about her marrying me. But she saw something in me that was worth the journey. So, a year later we were married and started pastoring a small church in Willits, Northern California. During those 11 years, Heather and I both went on a transformational journey together. I got an upgrade in Kingdom values for how marriage should be, how leadership should be, and many other relational dynamics.

Without Heather's kindness but firmness in having healthy foundations in our relationship, I wouldn't have made it to where we are today. Both of us have a huge passion to see people emotionally and relationally whole. Heather's upbringing caused her to have to reach out for emotional health and freedom in Christ. She was passionate to not allow unhealthy anger, codependency, unforgiveness, bondage, and fear be a part of our lives.

I'm so thankful God gave me such a wonderful gift in my wife. I am so proud of her and am so happy to introduce her to you. Some of you may already know her and some of you may not. But through this powerful journey through Heather's life, you are going to experience for yourself what true freedom looks like. I have watched Heather fight for her dreams, her children's dreams, my dreams, and many other people's dreams. She fights for people to be free to dream, but she does it in a way that doesn't hurt others.

Over the years, I've seen many women trying to be free. In doing so, I've seen some throw off their husbands, families, and other healthy relationships. They feel in order to be a powerful and free woman, they have to make sure they are stronger than the men and world around them. That is not healthy and that is not Heather. She is strong, powerful, and full of faith, but she is also kind, caring, and sensitive to others. She is a perfect match for me, cares about her family, and prioritizes their needs. She also knows the value of taking care of herself and her own needs and dreams and making them known to those who love her. She is a wonderful, healthy Kingdom model of a woman who is loved by God and the people who have the privilege of knowing her personally.

It is my joy and privilege to invite you into Heather's journey in this book. Read this book with your own transformational journey in mind, and know that you, too, are designed by God to be powerful, free, and healthy emotionally and relationally.

I'm excited to see what the Lord will do with every person that encounters God through this book.

With expectation,

Keith Ferrante

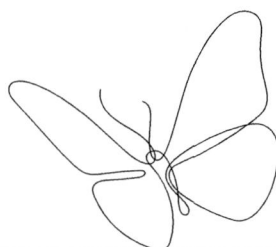

WE BEGIN OUR JOURNEY

THINKING THINGS WILL GO

A CERTAIN WAY, AND THEN

THINGS CHANGE, SHIFTING

IN A COMPLETELY DIFFERENT

DIRECTION ALL TOGETHER.

99

01

Change Your Story and
Change Your Life

"**I**F TIME OR MONEY WERE NOT AN ISSUE FOR YOU, what would you be doing right now and why?" My friend asked me this question one night and it really got me thinking. This is a question I have been asked many times in the past and has helped shape the course of my family's life. Now, it's a question I often ask others. At that particular time in my life, I was a bit perplexed. I was sensing a shift, but at the same time I was learning to enjoy and embrace the season I was in. Honestly it had been a while since I had visited this question for myself. Little did I know that when I finally came to grips with myself and answered the question, the wind would shift, the sails would turn and I would be headed in a direction I had convinced myself was impossible.

So many things in life and in the Kingdom start out one way but don't always end the way they began. Oftentimes, thoughts, ideas and dreams are given to us in seed form, but it takes many elements, one being the right environment, for it to actually take root and grow. This makes me think of the parable of the seeds in the Bible. Let's take a look at what it says in Matthew chapter 13.

> "That same day Jesus went out of the house and sat by the lake. Such large crowds gathered around him that he got into a

boat and sat in it, while all the people stood on the shore. Then he told them many things in parables, saying: 'A farmer went out to sow his seed. As he was scattering the seed, some fell along the path, and the birds came and ate it up. Some fell on rocky places, where it did not have much soil. It sprang up quickly, because the soil was shallow. But when the sun came up, the plants were scorched, and they withered because they had no root. Other seed fell among thorns, which grew up and choked the plants. Still other seed fell on good soil, where it produced a crop—a hundred, sixty or thirty times what was sown.'"

Everyone has the equal opportunity to receive a seed, but that seed needs the proper elements and right environment to grow into a beautiful healthy plant or tree.

Jesus then goes on to share what that parable meant:

"Listen then to what the parable of the sower means: When anyone hears the message about the kingdom and does not understand it, the evil one comes and snatches away what was sown in their heart. This is the seed sown along the path. The seed falling on rocky ground refers to someone who hears the word and at once receives it with joy. But since they have no root, they last only a short time. When trouble or persecution comes because of the word, they quickly fall away. The seed falling among the thorns refers to someone who hears the word, but the worries of this life and the deceitfulness of wealth choke the word, making it unfruitful. But the seed falling on good soil refers to someone who hears the word and understands it. This is the one who produces a crop, yielding a hundred, sixty or thirty times what was sown."

My husband Keith and I recently moved into a different house. The previous owners had a lemon tree out in the backyard planted in a pot, but the tree was pretty frail and the roots were exposed. It was positioned in a place that wasn't receiving much light. When I looked at it, I thought, *if I want lemons in the future, I need to make the needed changes to bring the tree back to life.* The tree had a few tiny lemons budding and some were already dried up and ready to fall off. The first thing I did was move it into the light and give it a good drink.

Next, I went to the local hardware store to pick up some potting soil so I could cover its roots and clipped off the extra dead limbs and leaves. I then began to watch and water it daily to see what would happen.

Within two weeks the lemons had at least doubled or tripled in size. This little tree appeared to be lifeless, but with a few quick changes it began to thrive and come back to life.

When we are born into this world, we don't have a choice as to which environment we are born into; we don't get to choose our family. With each individual comes a different story. Some environments are super loving, gracious and kind. Others are very broken, selfish, dysfunctional and downright mean. Without intervention and left on their own, people often become a product of the environment they were born into, however good or bad that may be. But one thing I know to be true is that despite the different stories we are each created with, we all have the same opportunity to choose a different outcome. If we don't like our story or the way things are for us, we can choose a different pathway.

We can change our story.

This reminds me of one of my favorite movies. Years ago, we took our kids to the theater to see a new movie called *Kung Fu Panda*. It's a lighthearted movie about a panda named Po. Po's big dream was to one day become a Kung Fu legend. In the movie, Po finds himself on a journey to find his true self. He searches everywhere to find his identity, his family and his place in the world around him.

Have you ever watched a movie and felt like the director was speaking directly to you? Something about this movie really captured my attention. Trust me, it's not every day that you pull out your phone and start taking notes and typing out specific quotes in the middle of a movie. But that day I did, and this is a quote I will never forget:

> "Your story may not have such a happy beginning, but that does not make you who you are. It is the rest of your life that does – who you CHOOSE to be."

Wow! That resonated with me on a very deep level.

Just because you were born into a situation that wasn't the best doesn't mean you must repeat the same unhealthy pattern. You can choose a different way for yourself and your family. There are so many resources and tools to help you undo mindsets and unhealthy patterns of living if you really want the help.

I think we get stuck here sometimes. Often, we don't think we have a choice. If we don't know any better, it can be easier to play the victim and do life as we've always known it rather than making the effort to do something different. Unfortunately, fear, insecurity and lack of trust holds us chained to a life we do not really enjoy.

But let me tell you, there is HOPE! You don't have to stay in that endless cycle that seems like it will never change. Doing something different is a lot of hard work, but if we truly want change, we have to choose to do it.

This was me. This was my story. I lived gripped with fear. I was afraid of everything – afraid to walk into a room and be seen, afraid to use my voice, afraid to say no, afraid to say yes. Early on, I recognized that living in fear was not the way I wanted to live my life. I didn't want to raise my kids in fear. I didn't want them to fight through the same battles I had growing up. There was so much fear in my life, and I was a product of my environment. I've heard it said, "You're always one decision away from a totally different life. So, what did I do? I made a choice to change the cycle.

Have you ever read the definition of insanity? Insanity is defined as wanting something different but doing the same thing over and over and getting the same result time and time again. It's kind of like that old song, "The Song That Never Ends" or maybe "It's a Small World" at Disneyland. As soon as you hear it, it gets caught on repeat in your mind and doesn't seem to stop.

Too many people are stuck on the hamster wheel of their own story. They believe the lie that there is no way out. Unfortunately, that becomes the reality for most people who believe the lie to be true. However, I know your story can be different if you let God help you. He's done it for me, and I know He can do it for you.

Through the years, many chapters are written in the storybook of our lives. Some chapters are brighter and bolder than others. Some may be very dark or even blank. Some chapters look more like a coloring book full of vibrancy and creativity, and other chapters may be torn out completely and burned as a way of trying to forget about them all together. For myself, I've found that many chapters were re-written once I reached a different phase in life.

We begin our journey thinking things will go a certain way, and then things change, shifting in a completely different direction all together. In the middle of it, oftentimes we don't see or understand why things happen the way they do, but if we give God the opportunity, He has the supernatural ability to create life and beauty out of the ashes of the burnt pages.

One of my favorite scriptures is in Proverbs 16:9: "A man's heart plans his way, but the Lord directs his steps." If we have committed to walking with Christ as the center of our lives, our story will probably end up a bit different than we had originally planned. I don't know about you, but that's been my reality.

Keith and I started leading a church shortly after we turned twenty-three years old. Looking back, I wonder how that was even possible. We were young, naive, super zealous and maybe a little ambitious. There were even times when we made really poor decisions. But God had a plan.

He took our hunger and our love for Him and each other to craft a beautiful beginning to the story of our lives. Without that beginning, we wouldn't have learned the valuable lessons we needed to learn in life to help us go the distance in our personal journey and walk with the Lord. As you continue to read this book, I pray that the stories I share from my life will help you gain a new perspective of hope and freedom and that your life will never be the same.

"Make Room"

"

A man's heart
plans his way,
but the Lord directs
his steps.

"

I SMACKED FEAR RIGHT IN THE

FACE, MOVED ACROSS THE

COUNTRY AND BROKE FREE

FROM THE CONSTRAINTS OF MY

CHILDHOOD AND INTO THE LAND

GOD WAS LEADING US INTO.

99

02
An Invitation to Leave the
Land of Familiar

'VE ALWAYS BEEN HIGHLY PERCEPTIVE. Even as a young child I was very aware of my surroundings and things that were happening around me. Whether in my home or somewhere else, my sensors were actively on and aware. The pressures of life were evident all around, and I always had a desire to make a difference and help bring about change. At a young age, I learned how to live life to please people. Fearing the consequences, I didn't want to get in trouble like other kids I knew, so I did whatever I could to be on my best behavior and peaceable. I learned how to walk on eggshells, walk the straight and narrow and perform well to avoid rocking the boat on any level. Nothing inside of me desired to experience any type of punishment. I was living afraid and completely full of fear.

This behavior followed me for many years and kept me from experiencing life to the fullest. I longed for freedom, but I was stuck and wasn't sure how I could get unstuck and be free.

Looking back, I'm pretty sure my subservient lifestyle didn't work out for me so well. Thankfully, God had a better plan and started me on a wonderful journey to find and experience His unconditional love.

His plan for me all along was to live a life of adventure that was full of freedom; true freedom only experienced through knowing Christ and having a personal relationship with Him. I am so grateful that God started bringing people into our lives who helped show us the way forward and set us on a new course of life and healing.

I grew up loving God and His church. When I was twenty years old, I moved away from home to attend Bible college. This is where I met and fell in love with my husband Keith. A year later, we were married with no place to live and no jobs. That sounds like a great way to start a marriage and ministry, doesn't it? Ha! Not quite. But hey, we were full of faith, had adventurous spirits and wanted to save the world, so at least we had something going for us.

Driving away from the church where we got married, we were in a rush, ready to get on with our married life just the two of us. But when we got in my car, it needed gas. I'm not sure why no one thought of filling our tank before we left, but nonetheless we were not going to make it to our destination without stopping for gas.

We pulled into the gas station and Keith glanced into the rear-view mirror. "Why is your dad pulling up behind us?" he asked. When I looked back, there was my dad, doing what a good dad would do. He chased us down to bring us something he knew we would need on our trip. He was carrying one of my pieces of luggage that was left at the church. Someone had forgotten to put it in the car. I was so grateful for my dad at that moment. As a new bride, I can't imagine showing up for our honeymoon without my makeup and bathroom bag. I was grateful to see him, and of course he ended up paying for our gas (an additional bonus).

Looking back, there were many things about our special day that we would now do differently. We had to drive over five hours to get to our hotel for the night. I'm not sure what we were thinking, but we were young, in love and ready to be in a hotel room just the two of us. Keith and I had "saved ourselves for marriage" and were ready to start our new life together as husband and wife. We also had an early morning flight waiting to whisk us away to our Hawaiian paradise where we would survive on .99 cent tacos and Tostito chips for the next ten days.

On the way to our hotel that night, our car overheated right after my new groom revealed to me that he'd told a pastor in the inner city of St. Louis we would accept a youth pastor position upon returning from our honeymoon. The car was not the only thing hot in that moment. Shocked, I didn't know what to think or how to respond to him. On one level, I was happy, because that meant we would be staying a little closer to our families who all lived in Missouri at that time. On the other hand, he didn't know that a dear family friend of mine had told me at our reception that we should seriously pray about whether or not we should accept that position because she knew the pastor and the situation we'd be walking into. To me that was a big red flag.

At this point, we were both tired, grumpy and ready to be at our hotel. We finally made it to Kansas City and settled in for our first night as husband and wife. We ventured off to Hawaii the next morning with so many questions. Where were we going to live? How would we pay for anything? Neither one of us had a job, we had zero savings, but now we had each other. Our honeymoon consisted of lots of crying, praying, Jack in the Box tacos and phone calls. Not exactly a new bride's dream, but I was in Hawaii with my new husband, and that's all that mattered at the time.

On our way back to Missouri, we stopped in San Francisco. A church in Willits, California, wanted to interview us for a youth pastor position. Now remember, we had already said yes to this other church in St. Louis, but we did have a few other opportunities we needed to rule out. Keith was very familiar with this church because it is where he grew up during his high school years. His parents had once pastored this same church. They had since moved to Missouri and another couple was pastoring at the time.

We arrived in San Francisco, and I wanted to get back on the airplane and go home. I was born and raised in the St. Louis area, and back then California wasn't that appealing to me, especially this little town tucked away in the Redwoods. The minute I arrived, it felt like we had gone back in time over thirty years. I was newly married, full of fear, and wasn't quite ready to move all the way across the country to a land filled with hippies and marijuana. I had so many thoughts when I got there. *What is this place? Did this city ever come out of the 70's? Why would I ever want to live here?* I was so naïve. *Could this actually be a place God would call us to?* I had prayed all my life, *God, I'll go where you want me to go. Send me!* Oh boy. What was I getting myself into?

We were greeted by the pastors, and they showed us all around. I was excited to see the place where Keith grew up, but reality was setting in: this place could actually become our new home. It was nothing like where I had grown up. I remember wiping tears from my eyes quite frequently the whole week we were there. I was newly married and afraid. *How will I ever fit into this place? How will I survive living so far away from my family?*

Sunday rolled around and the pastor asked me if I'd be up to singing a special song during service. Back then, we had tracks we'd sing along with in front of the congregation. I graciously declined, saying I hadn't brought any soundtracks with me. However, when we arrived on Sunday night, a woman walked up to me with a huge smile on her face, holding a large box of soundtracks. The pastor looked at me and said, "Surely there's a song in there that you know."

I looked through the box, and out of 50 plus cassettes, I knew one song. One! So, I agreed to do it. The woman took me back to the youth pastor's office so I could do a quick run through. Little did I know that God was setting me up to have a pretty significant encounter with Him. I sang through it really quick, not paying attention to the words, and then I heard the Holy Spirit speak to me. "Sing the song again, and this time listen to the words you are singing." In that moment, I knew what was happening. With the words to the song, I knew God was calling us to this place yet I was resisting. But when I listened to the song again, peace settled in my heart. *Lord, I know You'll take care of us.*

A month later, we left our land of familiarity and moved to Willits. These were some of the most difficult and most incredible years of our lives. We served as youth pastors for five months, and then we were voted in as the Senior Leaders. Was I afraid? Yes. Did I want to quit? More times than I can even write about in one book. But I did it. I smacked fear right in the face, moved across the country and broke free from the constraints of my childhood and into the land God was leading us into. Little did I know that God would use this move to be the beginning of my freedom story.

A TIME OF
Reflection

Have you ever felt like God was calling you to leave your land of familiarity? If so, what was God teaching you through this process? The land of familiarity doesn't have to be a geographical place. Oftentimes, it's a season of life or even a mindset. It's a place that's taking up space in your life; a place you've simply gotten used to or comfortable with.

"Beyond the Open Door"

Have you ever been in a place where you have resisted God? Take a moment and listen to the following song: "Beyond the Open Door." Ask God to speak to your heart and show you any areas where you may need to surrender to Him like I did. Write your thoughts below.

DECLARATIONS

If God is calling me into something, He will get me the tools I need for my journey.

I can do all things through Christ who gives me strength.

God is faithful to complete what He starts in me.

With God all things are possible.

I have what it takes to do what God is calling me to do.

THANKFULLY, GOD
HAD A BETTER PLAN
AND STARTED ME
ON A WONDERFUL
JOURNEY TO FIND
AND EXPERIENCE HIS
UNCONDITIONAL LOVE.

99

FEAR IS A LIAR AND A THIEF.

FEAR WILL ROB YOU OF

EVERYTHING GOOD IN YOUR

LIFE IF YOU LET IT.

99

03

Freedom or Fear:

It's Your Choice

IN THE PREVIOUS CHAPTER, YOU'LL NOTICE THAT I mentioned fear a lot. Even though I felt like I smacked fear in the face by moving across the country when we were newly married, in time I realized fear had deep tentacles in me, rooted in the seedbed of my mind and my belief system. To this day, every time I choose to face fear it brings a new level of freedom in my life, and I feel myself getting stronger. I want to be known as a woman of courage, one willing to fight for freedom for my family and the generations to come. That is my hope and prayer for you as you read this book. I pray that God would bring to light any fears you are facing and that you would encounter a fresh level of freedom through my story.

For many years, I have heard the saying *fear is not your friend*. That always sounded like a great statement to me, however that was not my reality. I wish I could say I've never struggled with fear, but that is not the case. As I mentioned, I was held captive by fear at a very young age, and it has taken me years to experience breakthrough in this area of my life.

Night after night, I would lay in bed being tormented by a spirit of fear. I would tremble and pray that it would go away. I would see things in my room, under the bed, in the dark hallway, and fear would pretty much keep me paralyzed. I kept a journal by my bed and wrote in it when I was afraid. I would write my prayers out to God (aka Truth), asking Him to help me- That is when I would find peace and finally fall asleep. As I got older and grew in my relationship with the Lord, things got better, but it has always been a struggle. Even though I knew all the Bible verses and would quote them out loud, the fear just wouldn't leave. Fear had become a dear friend of mine over the years, a stronghold without me even realizing it.

I remember my very first mission trip. I was ministering in the inner city in Los Angeles, California, with a team from Bible college. We had gone out to grab dinner, and as we were walking back to the campus where we were staying, it was getting dark. Out of the shadows, a few guys from a gang approached us. One of them had a knife, and I remember my whole life flashing before my eyes. My heart started to race, and the only thing I could say was, "God has not given me a spirit of fear, God has not given me a spirit of fear." I started walking as fast as I could as I repeated this scripture over and over, trying to take captive every negative thought racing through my mind. Of course, we made it back to the building alive thanks to a couple of the guys on our team who were willing to stop and have a conversation with the gang (and ended up leading one of them to Jesus). But fear gripped me that day and tried to steal the life and joy of that trip right out of me.

Fear is a liar and a thief.

Fear will rob you of everything good in your life if you let it. The Bible says in John 10:10, "A thief comes to steal, kill and destroy, but Jesus comes that we have life and life abundantly." The enemy is a thief. I want you to always remember that!

Second Timothy 1:7 also says God has not given us a spirit of fear, but of power, love and a sound mind. Fear does not come with the gift of love when we accept Christ into our lives, freedom does. Jesus is a picture of perfect love, and it's His love that sets us free and renews our mind.

Even though fear was familiar to me, I never wanted it to play the role of friend in my life. To this day, when I hear the saying *fear is not my friend,* I can attest that is true.

Who in their right mind would want a friend that constantly stole from them, lied to them or even set out to destroy their life? Friendship is about love, trust, caring and valuing one another. Fear should never be allowed to live anywhere near that boundary circle in our lives. However, for myself and many others it seems to be a common place where fear takes up residency.

Another word for fear is intimidation. Intimidation means to be a little less than who you really are. The enemy doesn't want you to be bold or courageous. He wants you to keep things dialed down. If the enemy can keep us afraid and intimidated, he knows we will never leave our mark on this world with the impact God has intended for us. That is his goal. He wants to stop us dead in our tracks, immobilize us and render us powerless.

However, there's good news: God has nothing but love for us, and love dominates fear. God gives us power, love and a sound mind. He gives us power to make wise choices, love to overcome our worst fears and a sound mind to keep us focused and at peace. Even though I didn't want anything to do with fear, I wasn't sure how to really get rid of it. How could something that had plagued me for so many years go away? I had lived with it for so long that it was very challenging for me to see my life without it. Even though I didn't want it and knew it wasn't from God, it took years for my mind to believe what my heart, spirit and leaders were telling me. Fear *wasn't* really my friend, and now I live to tell my story to help others escape the chains of fear and experience a life full of freedom. As we embrace the truth that God loves us, likes us and actually wants us to enjoy our lives, there is a door of freedom opened to us, leading us into a broad, spacious place.

I'll never forget the time when God showed me what fear looks like. As I share it, I hope it becomes a real visual for you like it did me. I pray that it brings breakthrough in your life.

I was in a worship service one day at the church we were pastoring at the time. We loved incorporating the arts in our services and had special stations set up for people to paint during our worship meetings. I was sitting in the back of the room on the floor by one of the art stations and had my eyes closed. I really wanted to paint during worship but couldn't muster up the courage to do it. I was really struggling with a lie: *I'm not an artist, and even if I tried it wouldn't be good enough to show anyone.* I had never painted in church before. In fact, it had been years since I had even attempted to do any kind of art. While I was praying and asking God why it was so hard for me to pick up the paintbrush, the Holy Spirit brought back a memory of being in sixth grade art class. Somehow, I had blocked this memory out of my mind.

Art was a required class back then. It was a class that I really enjoyed; it was on the top of my list of favorite classes (right next to my music class). One of our assignments was to sketch a tree. I remember working on my sketch, wondering if I was doing it correctly, but we were instructed not to ask for details. Just do the work. I pushed through all my questions and was happy with the way it turned out.

The next day when we were in class, the teacher started talking about the proper way to sketch this assigned tree, and then asked me to come up to the front of the classroom. I was so excited; I thought she was going to say something nice about my sketch, but when I stood next to her, she grabbed my drawing and showed it to everyone in the class and used it as an example of how NOT to draw a tree. It was heartbreaking and humiliating. That day I vowed to never do art again. It crushed my little spirit.

When I was reminded of this moment, tears filled my eyes. I felt ripped off and asked God to heal my heart. That night, I realized the *fear of man* stifled a God-given gift of creativity in me, and that made me mad. As I was sitting there worshipping, I had a movie-like vision that played out right in front of me. I saw this little, tiny imp-like creature standing by a brick wall in a dark alley. To the right of him was one of those giant spotlights, (you know the kind that shine giant lights up into the sky at night to draw you to an event.) The little thug kept positioning himself in front of the light to project an image of himself onto the wall behind him. The shadow looked huge and very scary. All of a sudden, I saw a giant hand come down from the sky. Immediately, I knew it was the hand of God. With one finger He smashed the little creature and it turned to dust, gone in an instant.

Peace settled in over my heart, and I felt the spirit of fear go. I picked up a paint brush that night. As God healed my heart and broke me free from that spirit of fear, my desire to create and paint returned. I started painting, and my first painting sold for $500. God cares about the things that are important to us. He created me to create, but the relationship I had with fear held me back from a part of my destiny for many years.

God is so good and faithful; He wants to bring healing and redemption to the things that hurt us on this journey of life.

Recently we decorated my husband's office wall with different art pieces and things that were special to him. A few of my paintings are on the wall, and one of them is a painting of a tree. I had never shown it to anyone publicly, but a friend and art mentor stopped by the house one day and we showed her around. She looked at the wall and said, "Oh, I really love that painting of the tree." She didn't know my story, but her affirmation instantly brought another level of healing to my heart. Years later, God is still redeeming things and bringing life to the things that the enemy meant for evil.

God gives us the power to overcome fear. He strengthens us with His Word and gives us relationships with people who have the ability to stand with us in the midst of fear and adversity. God's Word and promises are true. In Isaiah it says, "Do not be afraid. I am with you. Do not be terrified. I am your God. I will make you strong and help you. I will hold you safe in my hands. I always do what is right" Isaiah 41:10 (NIRV).

"

Do not be afraid. I am with you.
Do not be terrified. I am your
God. I will make you strong and
help you. I will hold you safe in
my hands. I always do
what is right.

"

A TIME OF
Reflection

Have you stopped doing something you were meant to do due to someone else's negative words or lack of sensitivity?

In which areas of your life does God want to bring restoration and freedom?

Take a moment and ask Holy Spirit to shine His spotlight of hope on your life today.

"No Longer Slaves"

Romans 15:13: Now may the God of hope fill you with all joy and peace in believing, so that you will abound in hope by the power of the Holy Spirit.

_____

_____

_____

_____

_____

_____

_____

DECLARATIONS

I am an overcomer!

God does not give me a spirit of fear, but power, love and a sound mind!

God cares about the things that are important to me.

My creativity doesn't have to look like everyone else's.

I am created to create.

My identity comes from the Lord.

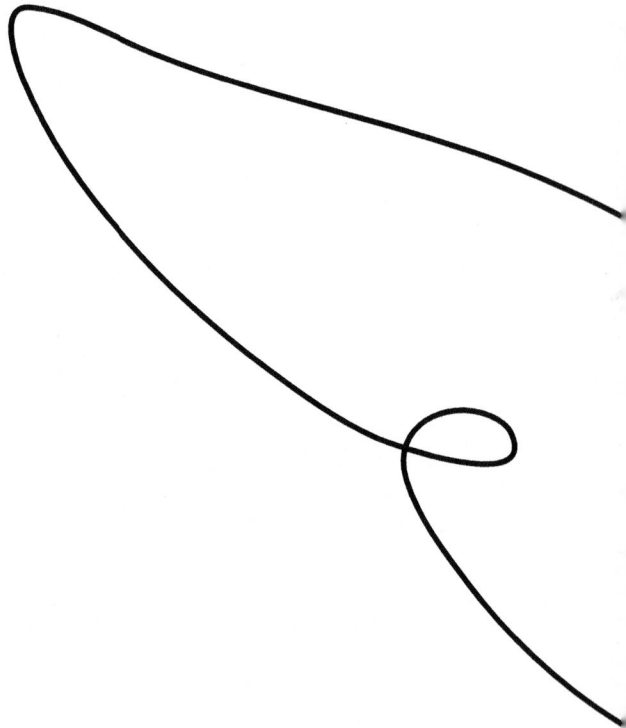

GOD GIVES US THE
POWER TO OVERCOME
FEAR. HE STRENGTHENS
US WITH HIS WORD
AND GIVES US
RELATIONSHIPS WITH
PEOPLE WHO HAVE THE
ABILITY TO STAND WITH
US IN THE MIDST OF
FEAR AND ADVERSITY.

99

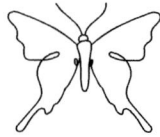

IT'S TIME TO BREAK AGREEMENT

WITH FEAR. IT'S BEEN HOLDING

YOU BACK FROM WALKING

IN THE FULLNESS OF YOUR

IDENTITY AND CALLING

FOR WAY TOO LONG.

99

04

It All Starts with
Your Yes

A S I WAS STANDING IN A MEETING TOWARD the back of the room, I heard someone behind me say, "You are a woman of great faith and courage." I remember looking around, trying to figure out who this person was talking to. However, I was the only one standing there. I said, "Who me?" They laughed and said it again. "Yes, you. You are a woman of great faith and courage."

I thought they were talking to someone else, because that was not something I believed to be true about myself. Notice my words here. *Those words were not something I believed to be true about myself.*

Courage is a choice. Courage is an action word just like faith is. "Faith is the substance of things hoped for, the evidence of things not seen" Hebrews 11:1. Courage and faith require action to please God.

Without faith, it is impossible to please God. If we are operating in fear, we are walking in the opposite spirit of courage and not operating in faith.

To believe in something or someone requires us to have faith in that person or thing. This often begins with our mindset. If we don't believe something to be true, then most likely it won't be true for us. Past experiences can dictate this cycle in our lives if we choose to let them.

For example, if we've known and experienced something a certain way for many years and someone challenges our thinking, suggesting that there might be a different way forward, our initial reaction often is disbelief. This is especially true when it's something you have never seen or hasn't been done before. Transformation happens when things change into something different.

If you do the same thing over and over and never try anything different, you're going to get the same results. However, if you are willing to step out and risk doing something different, your life could change for the better. Risk requires faith. Fear of change will keep you stuck in the same pattern you've always been in. The crazy thing is that fear often hides itself as wisdom, caution or loyalty. It suggests things like, "I'm not so sure about that. What if something goes wrong?"

But I want to ask you a different question: What if something goes right? What if your greatest breakthrough is actually on the other side of you saying yes?

Be transformed by the renewing of your mind. I love what the Bible says about this in Romans 12:2.

"Don't copy the behavior and customs of this world, but let God transform you into a new person by changing the way you think. Then you will learn to know God's will for you, which is good and pleasing and perfect."

Finding freedom requires you to take risks that lead to intentional action.

One of the things that can really help you along your journey is this: when you feel afraid to do something, be courageous and do it anyway. In Christ we are new creations. Fear didn't come with the package. "Therefore, if anyone is in Christ, he is a new creation; old things have passed away; behold, all things have become new" 2 Corinthians 5:17.

Courage takes action. Fear inhibits action. There's a big difference. Being a person of courage requires you to live intentionally and be willing to take risks that may not work out. It also requires you to smack fear in the face when it rears its ugly head, and then choose to keep moving forward regardless of how afraid you may feel. Fear is the complete opposite.

If you let it, fear will *always* intimidate you and hold you back from moving forward. It makes you question yourself. *Will I be accepted? Will I be received? What If people don't like me? What if I mess up?* Fear wants to keep you from your destiny. Let me ask you this: what are you the most afraid of doing? That thing you are most afraid of is probably a huge part of your destiny and calling. You might even find another level of breakthrough in your life if you take a risk and do it. True freedom says YES.

One day, after we returned home from living in another country for nearly three months, the phone rang; it was a dear friend of mine. She had planned a trip to go whitewater rafting on the American River near Sacramento, California, with a group of women. One of them had to cancel at the last minute, and she wondered if I might like to join her. It was the next day, and she asked me if I'd like to go. Before I even had time to think about it, the word YES jumped out of my mouth. I was actually taken back by my response because I'm not a huge fan of water and don't know how to swim very well. However, I did say yes and was excited to spend some time with her.

Honestly, I didn't really know what I was saying yes to. I had been on float trips before but never whitewater rafting. We arrived at the river, and I remember thinking *oh, this shouldn't be too bad. I can do this.* I was hopeful and up for an adventure, especially after doing life in Fiji for the past three months. The love for nature had grown in my heart.

All ten of us, including our guide, climbed into the big red raft. As the guide started giving us instructions for our upcoming adventure, I could feel fear start to rear its ugly head. This feeling was very familiar to me, but I was so over it. There was no going back on this one, and I had to consciously choose courage. The only way back to our car was to finish this whitewater adventure.

The first thirty minutes was smooth sailing, and then out of nowhere, our guide shouts out, "Brace yourself!" I thought I was going to pee myself. Fear gripped my heart like someone was trying to choke the life out of me. I panicked. I grabbed the side of the boat and slipped into the middle. "Everybody up on the sides of the boat!" I was the only person sitting in the middle of the boat in that moment, so I knew he was talking to me. Grabbing the handle on the side of the boat with all of my might, I sat back up on the edge. Through the rapids we went. I closed my eyes; I couldn't take it.

"Man down!" I heard the guide shout. I opened my eyes to make sure it wasn't me. Ha! I was so scared I couldn't tell what I was doing. One of the girls had bounced right off of the back of the boat. She was okay, but I was thankful it wasn't me. The rush of adrenaline I experienced in that moment was very real and there was no hiding it. I was terrified. When we got through our first rapids, we entered a section of the river where it was very calm and peaceful. I was quietly thanking God for the peace when an orange monarch butterfly flew right into the boat in front of me, and then flew away.

That was very significant. You see, we had just gotten home from living in Fiji for the summer. Our church leadership team sent us there to plant and lead their very first international ministry school. It was an amazing time for our family. God has often used a butterfly to remind me that He is with me, and ever since, butterflies have been a symbol of transformation and breakthrough to me. There were several times in Fiji when the Spirit of God would break out in a very special way and the presence of God was extremely tangible and life changing. Every single time that would happen, a butterfly would show up and fly around the room. This happened at least eight times while we were there. Years later when we went back, the same thing happened. At key moments, and at key breakthroughs, the butterfly would show up.

So here I was, being courageous, facing one of my worst fears (whitewater rafting), and after the first rapid a butterfly showed up. Coincidence? I don't think so. That butterfly flew right up to my face as to get my attention, and it did just that. I felt immediate peace as I watched it fly away over the smooth waters. God was letting me know He was proud of me and that He was with me.

Let me tell you about another time when God was helping me break the cycle of fear. I had taken a group of women to a women's conference where my friend was one of the speakers. The whole session was on overcoming fear, and this seemed to be a theme that God was dealing with in my life at the time. I was at the point of desperation. I needed breakthrough. I was so tired of this fear cycle repeating itself in my life.

As I sat in the afternoon session, listening to my dear friend, she shared about all of the different ways fear would show up in her life. She even struggled with making a left-hand turn while driving, afraid someone would hit her as she crossed traffic. To avoid this, she would go the long way around and make right-handed turns only. I listened to her stories of fear and freedom with tears streaming down my face. I felt like she and I were the only ones in the room, having a heart-to-heart conversation. In that moment, I was at another crossroads with this ugly monster that tried to keep a club of intimidation over my head.

At the end of her talk, she addressed the room. "I believe there are three different types of people in the room. The first group are the ones who acknowledge they have fear in their life, but aren't ready to deal with it. The second group are those who recognize they have fear and are comfortable enough to share that vulnerability with someone else and get prayer." But then there was a third group. She said the third group knows that *today is your day.* "You're over fear. You're done with this intimidation holding you back from walking in the fullness that Christ paid for. You want freedom, and you want it now. Run up here, and God is going to meet you today."

The feeling of fluttering butterflies was building in my stomach. I couldn't get up there fast enough. I ran up there and stood with my eyes fixed toward heaven. Tears wouldn't stop running down my face. As I waited for someone to come and pray for me, I started talking with the Lord. I prayed all the prayers of repentance, I sobbed my eyes out, and then heard the Lord speak to me. "Be still."

As I stood there in stillness, I heard Him quietly speak to me. It was as if He was giving me a conditional promise. This may seem silly, but in that moment, I knew God was speaking like He did to Naaman, instructing him to go down to the river and dip seven times to receive his healing. It was one of those types of moments.

I heard these words. "Heather, if you'll shout hallelujah as loud as you can, I'll break fear off of your life and bring you into another level of freedom."

You see, in that moment I began to wrestle with God. He and I were having a pretty intense discussion. Mainly me...I was talking, and He was listening to me make a bunch of excuses. Up until that point, worship music was playing pretty loudly. People were crying, laughing, falling down on the floor and truly encountering God and His freedom. People were experiencing breakthrough. It was amazing, and I was standing there in stillness (other than the conversation going on in my head).

Right before I heard God speak to me, the music changed to very quiet soft worship and everyone in the room became quiet and still. I'm thinking to myself, *God, it seems pretty insensitive for me to shout hallelujah right now. Do You not realize that? Literally everyone is still and quiet right now.* I wrestled with those words for what seemed to be an eternity. I kept trying to work myself up to it. I'd count to three and tell myself, *okay Heather, on the count of three you can do it, 1, 2, 3... nope, not doing it. 1, 2, 3...nope. 1, 2, 3...*over and over at least twenty times.

Fear was messing with me. It did not want to lose its grip on my life. It ruled and controlled me for years. But finally, I had enough, and out of my mouth came, "1, 2, 3, HALLELUJAH!" It was like I was the only one in the room and time stood still. There we were, just me and Jesus. I remember feeling such tangible freedom. I laughed, I cried and I fell forward on my face and laid on the floor for over an hour as God brought much needed healing and freedom to my heart. A team of leaders from the Mission Church in Vacaville, California, surrounded me, prayed with me and walked me through a process of freedom. It is a day I will never forget. It was life changing for me.

Have you ever felt the same way? Maybe you are in that place right now. If so, I invite you to ask the Holy Spirit to help you and bring a greater level of freedom. Which of the three categories above are you at today? Are you beginning to recognize that fear has had more of a grip on you than you've realized? Are you ready to share with a friend how you've been struggling and need more freedom? Or is today your day?

Why am I sharing my stories with you? To push back the gates of hell in your life. I wish I would have understood how reckless fear was early on. I know the pain of living in fear all too well, and it breaks my heart to see others bound by the grip of it when I know there is a greater reality available.

I'm inviting you into that journey of freedom right now. Are you ready? It's time to break agreement with fear. It's been holding you back from walking in the fullness of your identity and calling for way too long.

Father God, I'm asking that You would reveal Yourself as a good Father to every single person reading these pages right now, in Jesus' name. If they don't have an understanding of how good You are, I pray that You would bring healing to their hearts so they can receive that revelation. Lord, I ask You to show them how amazing they are, how much You love them and how much You are for them. I pray that Your Kingpin truth of freedom would replace fear's lies that they have been believing to be truth about themselves and others. Let freedom reign, Lord Jesus.

"

Lord, I ask You to show
them how amazing they are,
how much You love them and
how much You are for them.

"

A TIME OF
Reflection

Invite the Holy Spirit to take you deeper in your journey of overcoming fear. What does that look like for you?

In what areas have you been held captive by fear? Take a few moments to write them down below, and then ask God to show you what He wants to give you in exchange.

"Obedience"

DECLARATIONS

I am an overcomer.

God is always with me even if I don't feel Him.

Today is my day; it's my time for breakthrough.

I am courageous.

In Christ I am a new creation.

I LEARNED THAT
COURAGE WAS NOT THE
ABSENCE OF FEAR, BUT
THE TRIUMPH OVER IT.
THE BRAVE MAN IS NOT
HE WHO DOES NOT FEEL
AFRAID, BUT HE WHO
CONQUERS THAT FEAR.

—NELSON MANDELA

WE HAVE TO UNDERSTAND

WHEN IT'S TIME TO PURSUE THE

DREAMS IN OUR HEART OR TO .

WAIT FOR ANOTHER TIME.

99

05
Check Yourself Before
You Wreck Yourself

WHILE PASTORING OUR FIRST CHURCH in a small town in Northern California, it became evident that our hearts were enlarging for the *more of God* and our calling as young ministers. We began hosting ministers from around the world, and then were invited to travel with them. We went on a few different trips to South America and Europe, and our hearts were completely undone. We thought we had found our life's calling; it was amazing!

The favor of God toward us was over the top in these countries, especially Brazil. We would be ministering, and during worship people would come and lay gifts at our feet to honor us for being there. It was quite humbling. The leader we were traveling with told us he had been ministering there for several years and had never seen this happen before. He told us God was marking us with favor for the nations and our lives would never be the same. We fell in love with the people and the culture there. We honestly thought we'd head back home to California, pack up and move to Brazil to fulfill the call of God on our lives. Little did we know that God had another plan for us.

A few months after returning to California, I found out that one of my favorite missionaries was hosting a six-week mission training school in the heart of the slums in Sao Paulo, Brazil. Something leapt in my spirit like a kid in a candy shop, and I immediately wanted to go. I knew this wouldn't be easy and would require me to face some of my major fears, but I thought I was up for the challenge. I reached out to a few of our mentors, talked it through with my family and had the green light to move forward and attend. Little did I know that it would be much like Joseph in the book of Genesis, getting his coat of many colors, having a dream, receiving his calling, and then getting put into prison. There is always a distance between when the calling is revealed and occupying the office, but we obviously didn't have the revelation of this yet. However, this experience kick started a journey of growth that we are forever grateful for.

Here is a glimpse of what that experience was like for me and also the valuable lessons I learned from attending that school.

Holy Given

With the roar of helicopters flying overhead, it felt like I was in the middle of a CSI crime show. I was intrigued by the noise outside, so I looked out the window. The bars prevented me from seeing what was going on, but the next thing I knew, I was hearing gunshots and sirens. I quickly ran to my bunk away from the window, trembling with fear, not knowing what was really happening outside in this war-torn favela. The thin brick walls surrounding me were my only safe place at that moment. There was a war going on outside – a war for souls.

Upon arrival, we were each given a lime green vest to wear and were instructed to put it on every time we left the building. We were also told not to go down or even look at the street to the right of our building, due to it being a serious drug trafficking hub. Cameras and cell phones were not allowed to face that direction either. The drug lord was extremely active in this community and he wanted everyone to know that he meant business. However, he apparently appreciated the fact that the ministry we were working with fed the children of the community on a daily basis, so when teams of people came to help, he wanted to keep them safe.

To the natural eye, this place was not fit for children. But there they were...playing out in the middle of needle-infested and sewage-lined streets, wearing barely any clothes. Occasionally, I would notice a little toddler who had chunks of their ears missing due to their rat-infested living environments. I was completely undone. My heart was aching for these kids. No child should have to be exposed to this environment, let alone live there.

A cloud of fear loomed in this busy place where innocent lives were being stolen and sold for merely nothing. This was my life for seven weeks. We were there learning how to live and love the poor and the marginalized. The goal was to build relationships and trust with the locals in order to share the real, raw unconditional love of Jesus. Many of the young girls were prostituting themselves daily on the street where we lived. We had school during the day and outreaches in the afternoon. At least a thousand kids were fed weekly in this war-torn favela. I couldn't believe I was there.

A friend from our church went with me so I didn't feel completely alone. But our comfortable reality of living in California quickly shifted to living in the slums of Brazil amongst some of the poorest of the poor in the world. We ate beans and rice every day, showered with rain water, washed our clothes by hand in a concrete sink, and washed our dishes in cold water. At one point I thought I was going to die because of horrible food poisoning. My husband made me envelopes that had little notes in them for each day I was away. That became a lifeline for me while I was away from him and our two children.

Keith and I had been pastoring for over nine years at this time, and I was still hungry to grow in my calling as a woman in ministry. I was finally starting to come alive and was feeling free, except when it came to dealing with this stronghold of fear. For years I was afraid of everything that had to do with being seen or speaking. Being in the background (even singing background vocals) was comfortable. I had finally stepped into leading worship and had become comfortable being in front of people, but speaking in front of people was a completely different story. In my heart I wanted it. But every single time I would do it, a spirit of fear would literally grip me. I can remember having dreams where I would try to speak and the enemy would choke me; I would try to scream and nothing would come out. Night after night I was tormented by these dreams.

After getting a taste of the nations a few months prior, I was so hungry for more. So, when we found out that Heidi Baker was launching a branch of her mission school in Brazil, I instantly wanted to be a part of it. Heidi is one of my heroines in the faith and is known all over the world as being an Apostolic Mama of Love. What better place to be fully emerged in the love of God and face the giant of fear that had ruled my life, right? It was the ministry's first year of launching a school outside of their home country of Mozambique, Africa. Since we had a newfound love for Brazil, I was naturally drawn there. My hunger for true freedom was growing.

At this point in my journey, I had decided I was finally over dealing with this relentless spirit. It was constantly ruling my thoughts and my mind. I felt like I'd get a handle on it in one area, and then it would show up somewhere else. I would make decisions based on fear rather than truth. Determined to change my life, I was going to get rid of this thing once and for all. I knew that if I could face it, God would help me. I sought counsel from different mentors in my life and moved forward with attending the school.

I was there on a mission. I was there with a passion to face my own fears and find a greater sense of self awareness and purpose. Because I was hungry for more of God and wanted more of Him in my life, I was willing to do whatever it took to find it. As a mother of two children, leaving my family behind to live in a different country was not easy. I knew I would miss my family; however, I was desperate to know more about this God I read about in the Bible and was tired of fear gripping me at every turn. I wanted more for me. I wanted more for my marriage, children and generations to come.

The threats in my mind were very real and tormenting. I would hear things like, "If you go to Brazil I'm going to kill you and your family." The thoughts became visions where I started to see these worst-case-scenario things happening in my mind's eye. The plane I was going to fly on was tail spinning and crashing into the ocean or my team and I were lined up on the street getting shot at and killed. Visions of my family dying in a car accident would run rampant in my mind over and over again. It was absolutely terrible. I never thought I would make it through that foreboding fear. Even though I would take captive the thoughts they didn't seem to leave. In my mind, going to Brazil was exactly what I needed to face my fears head on. This trip happened to be just a few years after the 9/11 attacks when the Twin Towers and many lives were destroyed by terrorists using commercial passenger airplanes.

And of course, one of my greatest fears back then was flying. Fear seemed to be heightened at that time due to the recent terrorist attacks across our nation.

My first point of action would be booking my ticket to Brazil on the same airline the 9/11 terrorists hijacked in their attack on the World

Trade Center. I'm not sure anyone can understand how hard that was for me. The threats from the enemy through thoughts and visions were so real to me, but I came to the point where I'd had enough. To break the cycle of fear, I had to do the very things I was afraid of. So, I booked my ticket and off I went on an eight-hour flight.

Nothing about this trip was easy. It was one of the most difficult things I've ever done, and if it meant going to live in one of the most dangerous slums in the largest city of Brazil to do a mission school for seven weeks to overcome the fear of dying, it would be worth it.

One day while walking the streets during an outreach, I noticed things I wish I had never seen. There were men overseeing women and children in dark rooms making jewelry. They were working very fast, and something felt very off. I now know that what I saw was a front for what was really happening behind closed doors, but when I asked about it at the time, I was told to keep things quiet and they'd tell me more later. The later conversation never came. Apparently, this was normal. I knew this situation was bad, so I immediately took it to Jesus when we went back to the base where we were staying.

Grabbing my journal and pen, I plopped myself down on the dirt-lined concrete floor. I couldn't deny the sick feeling in my gut. My heart was aching for the people I had just seen on the streets. People should not have to live like this. I cried out and asked Jesus for a solution. He told me He wanted me to be a part of the solution, but I was clueless as to how that could ever happen.

As I started writing out my prayers, tears filled my pages so much that the ink started to bleed. I had a hard time seeing what I was writing, but I knew God was speaking. I wrote, then listened, and then wrote some more. He spoke very clearly that I had a mission field in my own backyard, and He wanted me to start there. *How could I ever start at home?* That didn't sound very exciting. It seemed much more fun to be traveling to the nations and seeing God's Kingdom expanded there. Little did I know that I was young and had a lot to learn.

My kids were six and four at the time, and I was a mom on a mission to pursue my destiny. We were senior pastors of a church and trying to do all the things. We wanted to make a significant impact on the world around us. We had started traveling the world and our heart for the nations was expanding rapidly. However, the pull for ministry seemed a bit more exciting than just staying home and being a mom. Although I loved being a mom, it seemed as though there was more reward in doing ministry. For whatever reason, I picked up that belief along the way somewhere in my journey. It makes me sad now to even think about how I could ever put ministry before my family, but back then, that was very esteemed. But God was in the process of changing my heart and ideas about what ministry really is and how unhealthy my view of it was.

As I was journaling that day, God started to speak to me about an outreach for kids I could do in my own city. He gave me the name "Willits Kids Club" and also a few people's names who would be helping me with it. The vision became clear, and I wrote it down. One of the people on the list was my sister-in-law Kristen. I was excited to share with her what I felt God was sharing with me when I got back to the States.

When I was able to share with her, she was excited with me but had bad news about the name Willits Kids Club. She told me we couldn't use that name. I was perplexed; God spoke to me about that name specifically. She mentioned that the local Boys and Girls Club had just changed their name to the Willits Kids Club, so we wouldn't be able to use it for our summer park outreach. I was bummed but came up with a different name to use and we launched "Gateway Kids" instead. We ministered to and fed several children and families that summer and had a great time doing it.

In the meantime, I was in the process of looking for a job. We had just purchased our first home and needed the extra income. Toward the end of the summer, someone mentioned that the Willits Kids Club was hiring a site director to start a new afterschool program at the local elementary school. There were several requirements that needed to be met in order to get the position, none of which I was technically qualified for, but God had a different plan. Because He mentioned the name to me in Brazil it gave me the courage to pursue this job. When God calls you to something He qualifies you.

I ended up being the best candidate for the new position and was hired on the spot. One of the best things about this job was that it was at my kids' school, and I was able to have them with me in my program. It also became one of my favorite jobs ever. God used my time in Brazil to re-position my heart and my priorities. God was first, but family (marriage and children) was designed by Him to be second; ministry was after those things were secure. I'm thankful for the lessons learned in Brazil. I found that it's important to pursue your purpose *while* being there with your kids. Being a mom is not a side hustle. It's a great joy.

Something in me changed that year. God did something deep in my heart during that season. I changed; my heart changed. When I returned home from Brazil I was a different person. Those seven weeks shifted something in me, and I could never go back to the old me. The change and growth in my life was exciting, however I wasn't expecting the response I was about to receive. Things became a little bit uncomfortable on the home front for a while.

Shift Happens

I was more than ready to see my family after living in the slums for seven weeks. They welcomed me with hand-painted Welcome Home Mommy signs and big smiles, especially from the kids. I ran up to them at the airport and put my arms around them with such joy in my heart, but their response was not the same, especially my husband's. I could tell he wanted to embrace me, but his body language was a bit stiff and seemed emotionally distant. I suddenly knew this was not the re-entry I was hoping for.

I could see the pain in his eyes. Not only had I changed the past seven weeks, but he had as well. We had a deep love for each other, that wasn't the problem. But back then, I was carrying the weight of many things. I pretty much ran the household, taking care of my husband and the kids' daily needs, plus paying all of our bills. Well, it was more like juggling the bills we needed to pay to try to make things work; we weren't exactly living within our means at the time. We had credit cards and used them often without paying them off at the end of the month. We were doing the best we knew, but were pretty clueless about how to be good stewards with our finances and definitely lived paycheck to paycheck.

Although the lessons we were confronted with during my trip to Brazil were very challenging, they taught us a lot and helped us to grow up. Would I recommend a young family to do the same thing now? No, absolutely not. At that point, we thought we were pursuing the call of God on our lives, but we were off in our timing.

You see, there are different times and seasons for everything. It talks about this in Ecclesiastes 3:1-8. Let's look at these verses together.

"To every thing there is a season, and a time to every purpose under the heaven:

A time to be born, and a time to die; a time to plant, and a time to pluck up that which is planted;

A time to kill, and a time to heal; a time to break down, and a time to build up;

A time to weep, and a time to laugh; a time to mourn, and a time to dance;

A time to cast away stones, and a time to gather stones together; a time to embrace, and a time to refrain from embracing;

A time to get, and a time to lose; a time to keep, and a time to cast away;

A time to rend, and a time to sew; a time to keep silence, and a time to speak;

A time to love, and a time to hate; a time of war, and a time of peace."

These two verses also apply:

Daniel 2:21 (ESV):

"He changes times and seasons; he removes kings and sets up kings; he gives wisdom to the wise and knowledge to those who have understanding..."

Psalm 31:15 (ESV):

"My times are in your hand..."

Even though I had some amazing breakthroughs facing and breaking free from fear at a greater level and gained great insights in the Lord and fresh revelation from Heaven as I was in Brazil, the timing of this trip was off. My passion for the nations was driving me. My priorities were out of alignment. The horse was behind the cart, pushing it forward rather than pulling it from behind. Looking back on this season of life I now realize how selfish it was for me to pursue ministry over my family. I didn't see this as a blind spot because it was a legitimate passion and calling that God had given me, but because I was out of timing, it nearly took me out of commission.

Timing is so important. Seasons are important. And learning how to operate within the correct season is important and brings freedom rather than bondage. Imagine it was thirty degrees outside. You're probably not going to run around in shorts and a tank top, right? If you're smart, you'll dress in the appropriate clothing so you can regulate your body temperature. You need to know what season you are in to enjoy it well and maximize your personal breakthrough. It's no different with being in the right timing.

The Bible uses the example of harvest in Proverbs 10:5:

> "He who gathers during summer and takes advantage of his opportunities is a son who acts wisely, but he who sleeps during harvest and ignores the moment of opportunity is a son who acts shamefully."

We have to understand when it's time to sleep and when it's time to harvest. We have to understand when it's time to pursue the dreams in our heart or to wait for another time. However, when it is the right season, it's important to take action.

I am so grateful for the powerful lessons both my husband and I learned from this experience. This trip very easily could have ruined my marriage and nearly did, but thankfully we had some great people around us to help us navigate the ups and downs. I didn't realize back then that my husband said yes to me going away for seven weeks because he believed in me so much; he wanted me to pursue the dreams in my heart. His heart was in the right place. We were there together in Brazil several months prior and both experienced extreme favor and blessings from God and the people there. We both felt called to that nation and were excited about the opportunities God was opening up for us around the world. So, he agreed to me going on one hand, but on the other he had some real needs and real questions about whether or not he could handle everything while I was away for that long.

We were senior pastors of a church, young and married with a full-on sex drive and our kids were young. That wasn't the best time for a wife and mom to be away. But we learned from our mistake and now can help others see that the grass isn't greener on the other side – even when it comes to ministry dreams and desires.

Your marriage and children should always come first after your personal relationship with Jesus. And when you honor God with prioritizing those covenants, He will bless you. Matthew 6:33 says, "But seek first the kingdom of God and His righteousness, and all these things shall be added to you."

Despite the poor timing, many good things came out of my time in Brazil in relation to our family getting stronger. We learned the lesson of prioritizing our family. We also learned that I was carrying way too much of the load and daily responsibilities as a wife and mom; I needed help. Both Keith and my priorities had to change to make our marriage, family and ministry work. We both loved the Lord with all of our hearts, that was never in question, but getting all things to work together for our good was another story. When we made the shift, we opened up a whole other level of freedom. It took us a good year to sync up with the new rhythm, but as soon as we did, our season changed.

God cared so much about our family that He gave me a plan to create a work environment that would let me have my kids with me at work. This not only impacted my immediate family, but also multiple families in the city where we were pastoring at the time. If we trust Him to guide our path, things work out much better than we could ever think or imagine.

God had many adventures ahead for our family, but we weren't ready for them yet. God was giving us a taste of what our reality could be if we chose to accept the mission. The tension of living in the present and knowing what God has promised up ahead isn't easy. But when you get a taste of God's reality for your life, it's worth the wait, and new and exciting adventures are sure to come along the way.

A TIME OF
Reflection

What areas do you need to grow in trust with the Lord? What areas have you struggled with in regard to timing? Share your thoughts, and then ask God to speak to you; write down what you feel He is saying to you.

Take the Priority Test for Healthy Relationships

Between 1-10, rate yourself: 1= not great, 10 = you're doing amazing

"The Father's House"

1. Do you have great mutual communication?

2. Do you know the love-tank needs of your family?

3. Do you prioritize building relationships with your spouse (if you have one) as the most important relationship to you?

4. Do you spend strategic weekly time with each of your children (if you have children)?

5. Do you value your spouse's input?

After taking the test, ask God if there is any place where you need to shift your priorities.

....

....

....

DECLARATIONS

There is a time and season for everything in my heart.

God's timing in my life is perfect.

I'm not going to miss out on God's plan by putting my marriage, family and relationships first. Prioritizing those things will help me go the distance in my life and calling in Christ.

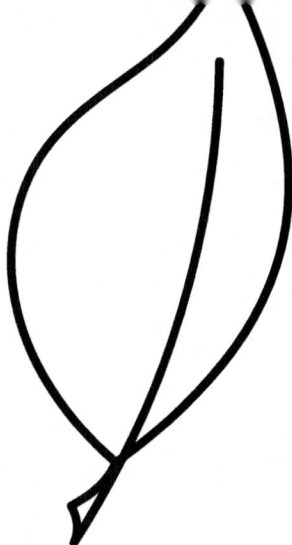

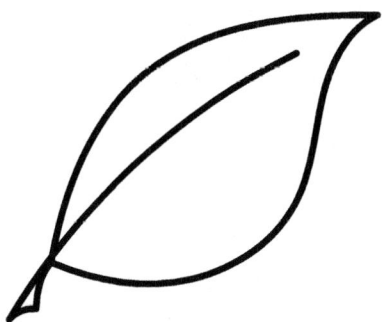

WHEN YOU GET A TASTE
OF GOD'S REALITY FOR
YOUR LIFE, IT'S WORTH
THE WAIT, AND NEW AND
EXCITING ADVENTURES
ARE SURE TO COME
ALONG THE WAY.

99

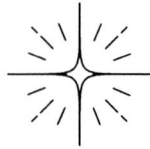

YOU ARE VALUABLE.

YOU ARE POWERFUL.

YOU MATTER. YOU ARE

GOD'S MASTERPIECE.

99

06
You Are God's
Masterpiece

TRUE FREEDOM COMES FROM KNOWING you are unconditionally loved, accepted, and valued by God Himself.

The key to sustaining any breakthrough you get in your life is learning to embrace and believe this truth. Don't take my word for it. God speaks it in His Word in Mark 10:27: "For with God all things are possible." Also, in Mark 9:23 it says, "All things are possible for him who believes." When we start to believe this truth, anything can become possible in your life.

Let me dive into this a little deeper. I know this can seem like an elementary topic, but it really is the anchor to our Christian faith. Let me explain it this way. You are the only person in the entire world who can add your unique value and expression to the canvas of life. What does this mean? It means without you and your input; the very texture of life's fabric would not be the same. You are valuable. You are powerful. You matter. You are God's masterpiece. Your story has the ability to change atmospheres and bring transformation to others whenever you share it.

I've heard it said time and time again, God made you an original, so don't die a copy. When we are growing in our gifting and grace, it's very normal to learn by copying someone. I know that many artists do this while learning to paint. They study how the master artists create a beautiful work of art and learn certain techniques from them. However, it is not normal to *stay* a copy. Over time, if you are persistent with practicing and pursuing your personal growth, your unique self and style will start to emerge and you will begin to leave your mark on the world around you.

For example, when my children were little, I would find them walking around the house in my shoes. They looked so cute. They would watch my husband and I do different things and would imitate our actions. My daughter had a fetish with getting into my makeup drawer. She would smear lipstick all over her face in an attempt to put it on her lips like I did. Why? Because they are watching and learning. They are growing. They try to implement what they are seeing. As they grow up, things change for them and they are able to implement what they have seen us do in their own way.

One morning, my husband and I were on a Zoom call teaching an online course. We were looking at the different people on the call and asking the Lord if He had a special word for anyone. One lady in particular stood out to me. I didn't think I had anything profound for her, but I called her out and said these words: "You are valuable, and you are powerful." I felt it so strongly over her, so I said it several times. Those words didn't seem profound to me, but to her it was life changing.

Shortly after I gave her that word, she reached out to me to share what that moment meant to her. She told me that she ended up writing a book, starting a business, and also starting a publishing company. Those words gave her the courage she needed to pursue the dreams in her heart. You never know the full impact of the words you speak to others. Your words are valuable and powerful and leave a lasting impact on others. The Word of God says that the power of life or death is in your tongue (Proverbs 18:21).

Proverbs 16:24: "Kind words are like honey – sweet to the soul and healthy for the body."

Proverbs 18:4: "A person's words can be life-giving water; words of true wisdom are as refreshing as a bubbling brook."

In another course I was teaching online, I had a lady who was struggling to feel beautiful. On day four of the course, she messaged me and shared about how she noticed her countenance had drastically changed over the past four days. She claimed that she looked ten years younger. After seeing some before and after pictures, it was absolutely true! Our words have the ability to change atmospheres in people's lives and bring life and freedom!

Let's take a moment and look at Merriam-Webster's definition of the word masterpiece. I love it. The word masterpiece means:

"The most outstanding original piece of work of a creative artist. An outstanding work, achievement, or performance. The very best. An original piece of artwork is the most expensive. It has the most value."

The Bible says this in Ephesians 2:10 (NLT):

"For we are God's masterpiece. He has created us anew in Christ Jesus, so we can do the good things he planned for us long ago."

When God created you, He had something very special in mind...you! He made you unique and everything about you matters. That means you are not ordinary or average; you are a one-of-a-kind original. God is proud of you and of what He made. He went to great lengths to make you exactly the way He wanted you. You're not meant to be like everyone else; God designed you the way you are for a purpose. God made you to be you, and you are the only one who can be you. I love what the Bible says in Psalm 139:13-18:

"You created the deepest parts of my being
    You put me together inside my mother's body.
How you made me is amazing and wonderful.
    I praise you for that.
What you have done is wonderful.
    I know that very well.
None of my bones was hidden from you
    when you made me inside my mother's body.
    That place was as dark as the deepest parts of the earth.
When you were putting me together there,
your eyes saw my body even before it was formed.
You planned how many days I would live.
    You wrote down the number of them in your book
    before I had lived through even one of them.
God, your thoughts about me are priceless.
    No one can possibly add them all up.
If I could count them,
    they would be more than the grains of sand.
If I were to fall asleep counting and then wake up,
    you would still be there with me."

When God looks at you, He sees greatness. He sees beauty and divine potential. You are His priceless work of art. When you understand your value—not only who you are, but also whose you are—then you will love yourself more and you will be able to love the people around you in a greater way. Because you belong to Him, you are extremely valuable.

When we were pastoring our first church, I didn't have the revelation of this yet. We were young, newly married, and trying to figure out life. I loved God deeply and tried my best to hear and listen to His voice.

One Sunday morning, I walked into my closet and asked the Holy Spirit what I should wear that day. My eye was immediately drawn to this beautiful, black two-piece suit. It was one of my favorite dresses, and I felt pretty when I wore it. It had three large silver buttons down the front, black fur on the lapel and cuffs and was a bit fitted. It was a suit I would wear on the holidays or for a special occasion. I immediately asked, "Holy Spirit, is the dress for today?" The answer was yes. As I was getting ready, I heard Holy Spirit whisper, "I want you to wear your red lipstick as well."

Red lipstick? I was a bit shocked. You have to understand something; I felt confident when I would wear this dress, and wearing red lipstick was pretty normal for me, but that morning I felt afraid. The fear of man gripped my heart. *What are these people going to think of me as a pastor wearing this outfit?* We were still fairly new to this church community, and I was having a hard time fully being myself. The fear of man was very real to me in that season. Growing up, I dressed up for church every week. I'd wear the gold shoes, big-brimmed hat, the works. That was normal for me, but that was the church culture in Missouri. However, when I moved to California, the culture was very different than I was used to. I argued with the Lord a bit before I fully committed. But one thing I know is that when God speaks, I want to listen and be obedient. So, I put the dress and lipstick on.

That morning I walked out of the church parsonage into the building feeling completely uncomfortable. I was ministering on stage with my husband, so everyone could see me front and center. Somewhat embarrassed, there I was, but something happened after service that altered my thinking.

A beautiful woman with short platinum blonde hair walked up to me and asked to speak with me. I didn't know her. She introduced herself to me, and said, "I need to tell you something." She proceeded to thank me for dressing the way I did that morning. I was in shock. Then, she said, "And your lips...you wore red lipstick!" She then proceeded to tell me that because I chose to be obedient and show up as my true self that day, it gave her the courage to do the same.

That day marked me. I'll never forget it. I felt the pleasure of the Lord that day and never thought twice about wearing that dress or lipstick whenever I wanted to again.

As we begin to change our mindsets and start to believe the truth of what God really says about us, our lives will drastically change for the better. This is the place where our identity becomes rooted in Christ. Once we start to believe and recognize this, our identity becomes the source by which our power and authority flows. Just think...what could happen if you truly believed you were as powerful as God says you are?

> *Our identity becomes the source by which our power and authority flows.*

I once read a story about a little old man who lived in a small run-down apartment building. He ended up dying in extreme poverty. At one point in his life, he was homeless and living on the streets. This man never had any earthly success to speak of or any noted victories. He lived and died as just another face in the crowd.

After he passed, some of his family members went to his apartment to clear out his belongings. There was a very small painting hanging on the wall and none of them wanted it, so they decided to sell it at a rummage sale.

The woman who purchased the painting from them thought it would be a good idea to take it to a local art gallery to get it appraised. In doing so, she learned that a famous artist who lived in the early 1800's had painted this small painting. She was astonished to find out the painting was extremely valuable. The woman auctioned off the painting and ended up selling it for several million dollars. That painting changed her life in an instant.

Just think how that poor man's life would have changed if he had known the value of what he had possessed. That poor man was a multimillionaire and didn't even know it!

His story captured my attention in so many different ways. So many people today are living with priceless treasure inside of them, and they don't even know the value which they possess. Some will even go to the grave without knowing because they are not willing to accept God's truth in their lives.

I'm always intrigued when I go into an art gallery. When my husband and I lived in Northern California, we would often visit art galleries in the Napa Valley when we would go there to have a meal. One day, we were in a gallery looking around and Keith stepped down into a different room. He came and got me and said, "Hey, guess how much this little painting is?" My random guess was way off. I think I guessed a couple of thousand dollars.

He said, "Nope, try again." I guessed wrong again.

He said, "How about $25,000 dollars?" I think my jaw hit the floor; I couldn't believe it. Questions began to fill my mind. *Why would this tiny painting be worth $25,000?* There had to be a story behind it, so we asked.

Apparently the guy who painted it had painted a few portraits of royalty, and the queen of that country found out and purchased them. Immediately, he went from being an obscure artist to someone whose art started selling for tens of thousands of dollars. Why would this happen? The price that the queen paid for his art determined the value of his work.

Think about that for a minute. If someone can go from being a starving artist to making lots of money selling his art just because of one transaction with the queen, how much more are we worth as sons and daughters of the King of Kings? Jesus paid the ultimate price for our salvation, healing and freedom. When He died for us so that we could walk in the fullness of our identity in Him, Jesus set the value for our lives. He wants us to receive that for ourselves.

"

What could happen if you
truly believed you were as
powerful as God says
you are?

"

A TIME OF
Reflection

Take a few minutes and quiet yourself before God. Ask Him to share three things about who He says you are. As soon as you have at least three things, take a moment and write down what He is saying.

"No One else"

When you have finished, take a moment to set aside everyone else's opinions of you and focus only on what God is saying. Pay attention to your emotions. How does what He says about you make you feel? What is He showing you about yourself that you haven't realized in the past?

When seeds of doubt and lies come into your mind about who you think you are or aren't, I challenge you to do this exercise as a reminder that what God speaks is truth over your life.

....

....

....

....

....

....

DECLARATIONS

I am God's masterpiece, an original work of art.

Jesus paid the ultimate price for my life, healing and freedom.

God sees me and knows my name.

All things are possible to those who believe.

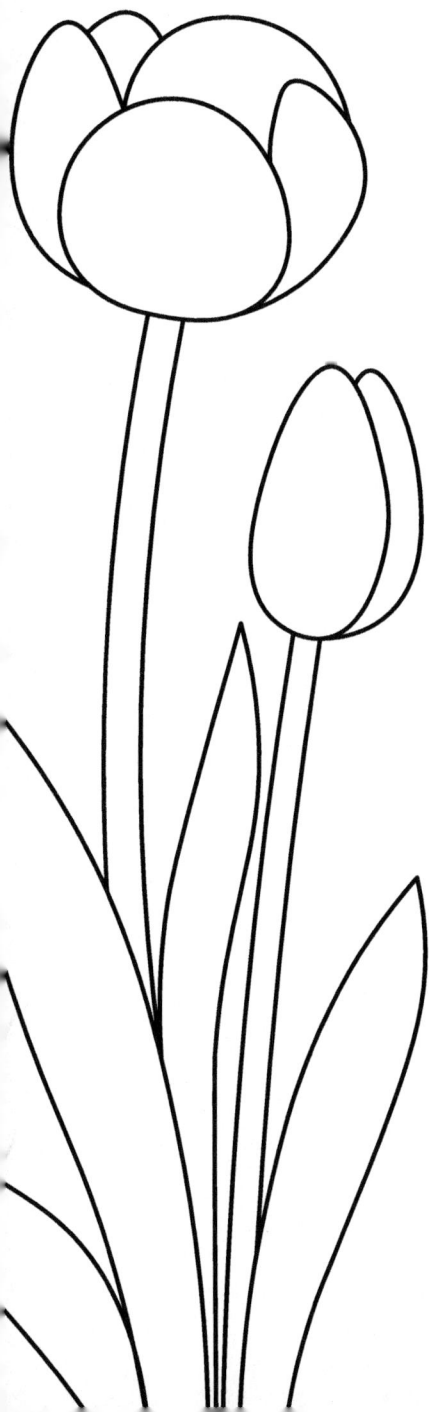

WHEN HE DIED FOR US
SO THAT WE COULD
WALK IN THE FULLNESS
OF OUR IDENTITY IN HIM,
JESUS SET THE VALUE
FOR OUR LIVES. HE
WANTS US TO RECEIVE
THAT FOR OURSELVES.

99

UNDERSTAND YOU ARE

IMPORTANT, AND OUT OF YOUR

IMPORTANCE, KNOW THAT YOU

ARE CALLED TO ADD VALUE TO

THE WORLD AROUND YOU.

99

07
Understanding Your
Identity and Purpose

ONE OF THE THINGS I LOVE TO DO WITH people is to help process their prophetic words and then craft an identity statement out of them. Years ago, we learned how to do this with different mentors and leaders in our lives, and it has been a great tool for us in life and ministry. Let me give you an example of what I mean. If you ever have an opportunity to receive a prophetic word from someone, I encourage you to do two things: grab your phone and record it, and then take the time to transcribe the recording. It's really helpful to have words recorded because it's easy to forget things the first time we hear them. If you don't have a device to record, then simply write the word down. My family and I personally type out our personal prophetic words with double line spacing so that they are easier to read. Also, it gives me a good amount of room for writing notes.

Print out two or three different prophetic words you have received in the past. If you only have one, it will still work; print that one out. Go through each of those words and highlight anything that stands out to you, specifically circle things that speak specifically to your identity—words that describe who you are as opposed to what you do. As an example, let me share one of my prophetic words with you. In this example, I circled identity words and underlined words that talk about what I can or will do so that you can see the difference.

> Heather, I see you as a (woman of prayer.) Your prayers are (powerful) (and effective.) When you pray atmospheres shift and big giants are taken down. (You are a mother) who has a high value for purity, and (you are loved and highly favored.) You are a (mentor) who will release generations of revivalists. People feel safe and receive direction when they are around me. You are a (declarer of truth and) understand times and seasons. You are a (creative worshiper) and have been created for Kingdom business. You carry an anointing for (beauty, style, and grace) and help women discover that for themselves. (You are wise) beyond your years and bring hope to restore people's dreams and destinies.

After you go through each of your prophetic words and make notes, list the things you circled that speak about your identity. When you finish this, craft an identity statement from this list. Declare this identity statement over yourself until you have it memorized and fully believe it!

Here's an example of what my identity statement looks like based on this exercise.

I am Heather.
I am a powerful and effective woman of prayer.
I am a mother who values purity.
I am loved and highly favored.

I am a mentor, releasing generations of revivalists.

I am a declarer of truth who understands times and seasons.

I am a creative worshiper.

I am anointed for beauty, style, and grace.

I am wise beyond my years.

I am Heather.

By doing this exercise, you will gain clarity on what God says about you. This gives us definition of our God-given identity and purpose. When we define ourselves by what God says about us and who He says we are, we get an upgraded perspective and are able to see ourselves the way God sees us. When this happens, there is healing, renewed life, a sense of direction and clarity of purpose. When all of these things are working together and are aimed in the right direction, we become unstoppable.

One of the biggest stumbling blocks I see for people who want to move forward in their destiny is that they get stuck defining themselves by what they do. They get caught up in their title, their position, and/or their activities. Oftentimes people gain a false sense of identity by doing this, and when they are no longer doing that certain thing or job, their whole world falls apart. If we allow ourselves to anchor our hearts and our identity to "that thing," we feel lost when it is no longer what we are doing.

We cannot afford to define ourselves by what we do. When we come into agreement with and choose God's thoughts for our lives, nothing else seems to really matter. We begin living for an audience of One, and the expectations we put on ourselves, the fear of man and the spirit of comparison is displaced in our lives, giving God the ultimate place on the throne of our hearts. If you don't understand your value, you may be thinking things like this:

I'm just average; I can't do this.

_____ can do it better than me.

I'm not that talented, so why should I even try?

My words hit the floor when I try to speak; my voice doesn't really matter.

I've made so many mistakes, how could God truly ever really love me, and how could others believe in me?

Have you ever had any of these thoughts running through your head? I know I have, and I know I'm not alone.

Understanding exactly *whose* you are and how you fit into God's plan creates such freedom, purpose and confidence. You are a person of destiny. You have an assignment, and you are full of gifts, talents, encouragement and love. You have rich treasure inside you that people need. You have more in you that you realize, and you can accomplish more than you ever thought possible. Dare to be bold and believe that you are a person of destiny; when you do, you will leave your mark on this world. Understand you are important, and out of your importance, know that you are called to add value to the world around you.

No matter where you are in life today, you have potential to increase, grow, be strengthened, and to move forward. God created you for His good purpose, so know beyond a shadow of a doubt that you are His masterpiece!

"

God created you for His good
purpose, so know beyond a
shadow of a doubt that you
are His masterpiece !

"

A TIME OF
Reflection

What are some areas where you've struggled to believe the truth about yourself? What lies have you believed that keep you from walking in the fullness of your destiny in Christ?

What is God speaking to you as you read this chapter? What has God spoken over you? What does He call you?

"You Say"

After you answer those questions,
I encourage you to craft your own identity statement and write it out below.

_____

_____

_____

_____

_____

_____

_____

DECLARATIONS

I am valuable and have purpose.

My life matters.

I have the strength to stand and be strong in the midst of difficult situations.

I am filled with the wisdom it takes to make good decisions.

In Christ, I am equipped with everything I need.

My voice is powerful and leaves ripples wherever I go.

NO MATTER WHERE YOU
ARE IN LIFE TODAY, YOU
HAVE POTENTIAL TO
INCREASE, GROW, BE
STRENGTHENED, AND TO
MOVE FORWARD.

99

I PRAISE YOU BECAUSE I AM

FEARFULLY AND WONDERFULLY

MADE; YOUR WORKS ARE

WONDERFUL, I KNOW THAT

FULL WELL.

99

08
Slaying the Giant of
Comparison

W E LIVE IN A CULTURE OF CONSTANT COMPARISON. Every single day we compare things without realizing it. We compare products when making a purchase, whether it be a major purchase such as a home, or a new vehicle, or a smaller purchase such as a new book, or even a loaf of bread. It's no wonder that it's something we can easily struggle with.

We say things like, "The cover on this book doesn't look as professional as this other one, so I think I'll get this one instead." We do this without taking into consideration what the actual content is all about. What about when we go to the grocery store and scrutinize the products? Is this bread gluten free, or does this product have dairy? It will either get put into our shopping cart or back on the shelf. We compare items that are similar, read every review we can get our hands on, and then we make a choice. I'm not saying options are bad, I'm just saying comparison is something all of us do.

If we hear or see anything negative, we often completely discount that thing and move on to the next. Each of us compare things on a daily basis, and it doesn't stop with things; we also compare ourselves.

So, let me ask you this. Have you ever compared yourself to another? Yes, I've done it; you've done it; we all have done it. We compare and judge others sometimes without even realizing it. Society looks at each other's outward appearance and automatically puts them in a specific social category. People are sized up by what they look like in a few seconds and not even given a chance otherwise, and we wonder why there are so many problems in the world around us (especially with our youth).

This is something I have struggled with on and off for several years. I grew up in a family where my dad was half Filipino and my mom was white. I am the first-born and am extremely fair skinned. My sister is the youngest, and she was born with dark skin. I always wanted darker skin because I felt like I would be prettier with a tan. I would go to the beach, lay in the sun, and by the end of the day I would be as red as a lobster and completely miserable. It's no fun being sunburned, and I definitely didn't achieve the "pretty" status I had in my mind by turning into a lobster.

Years later, I started traveling to the Philippines. I'll never forget the first time I walked into a store there and saw "whitening cream" on the shelves, just as we in America have tanning cream. Tears welled up in my eyes and my heart felt sad when I saw this. Something shifted in my heart that day. I realized that I had been comparing myself with others and losing my joy. The grass is never greener on the other side of the fence. God loved and created me the way I am, and I needed to embrace it.

So, years and many sunburns later, I finally gave up, threw my hands in the air and said, "I embrace my whiteness." It felt silly, but it was truly coming from my heart.

I love what the Bible says about comparison. Galatians 6:4-5 in The Message translation says this:

> "Make a careful exploration of who you are and the work you have been given, and then sink yourself into that. Don't be impressed with yourself. Don't compare yourself with others. Each of you

must take responsibility for doing the creative best you can with your own life."

Romans 12:5-6, also in The Message translation, says:

"In this way we are like the various parts of a human body. Each part gets its meaning from the body as a whole, not the other way around. The body we're talking about is Christ's body of chosen people. Each of us finds our meaning and function as a part of his body. But as a chopped-off finger or cut-off toe we wouldn't amount to much, would we? So, since we find ourselves fashioned into all these excellently formed and marvelously functioning parts in Christ's body, let's just go ahead and be what we were made to be, without envy or pridefully comparing ourselves with each other, or trying to be something we aren't."

I truly believe that comparison is one of the greatest thieves we can face when it comes to growing in our walk with God.

James 3:16: "For where jealousy and selfish ambition exist, there will be disorder and every vile practice."

John 10:10: "The thief comes only to steal and kill and destroy; I came that they may have life, and have it abundantly."

The enemy knows how powerful you are as a son or daughter of the King. However, he doesn't want you to recognize it or take ownership of it. He is afraid of you stepping into the fullness of your identity and authority because it means sudden death to him.

I remember one of the first times returning to the Fiji Islands after living there for a few months with our family the year prior. One of the ladies who was a part of our ministry school ran up to me, gave me the biggest hug and said thank you! "Thank you for teaching me U.B.U.," and then she shared a testimony with me.

While we lived there, I spent time hosting a creative workshop with a handful of the Fijian ladies. We painted traditional tapa, and I talked to them about how God has special gifts and creative talents for all of us. I talked to them about how no one in the world could do what they do the way that they do it. And then I said, "Oo boo" (U.B.U., aka you be you) because you're the only one who can. That's a fun little saying that I use to get people to remember *you be you*. Somehow it always sticks.

In Fiji, there are several traditional crafts that are known in specific regions. But if you don't live in the region, you typically don't do that craft. However; I encouraged them to try different crafts that they enjoyed and explore the things in their heart. The girls had never felt permission to do that before. I talked to them about becoming a resource and how God wanted to bless the works of our hands with finances to fund the things in our hearts.

One of the women had never painted before, but discovered she really had a gift for painting. She really enjoyed it. When we left the islands, she took the things I shared with her and got to work. She started a business of painting the traditional wedding garments. By doing so, she earned enough money to send her son to a special-needs school that he really needed but their family could never afford. By discovering what she had in her hand, she was able to change her family's trajectory and history. When she started believing who she was and what God said about her, and came into agreement with the fact that she was creative, she took a step forward into the land of risk. By doing this, it opened up a new realm of opportunity for her and her family. Her dream could now become a reality.

Another woman from the workshop shared with me how she wanted to become one of the first female prophetic trainers in the nation of Fiji. When she shared this, we were out on a boat traveling to the far outer islands to do some prophetic ministry. This trip opened up a new opportunity for her to teach on the prophetic. As we stood there and she was sharing this dream with me, she pulled out a little keychain. It had a boat on it, as well as a little dolphin and a little airplane. She told me that years ago someone had given her the keychain with a prophetic word about traveling on a boat and a plane to minister. She realized her dream was becoming a reality that weekend, and she was believing that one day she'd travel to America to do the same. A few years later, she found herself training in the prophetic and traveling to America. She even got to stay as a guest in my home.

God's Word is true, because He is truth.

Sometimes we have a hard time believing the truth, and when we come into agreement with doubt, we give up our authority. So, if the enemy can get us to walk in this spirit of comparison and competition with one another, he knows it will knock us out of our place of authority and leave us scrambling in the realm of jealousy and selfish ambition.

For years I compared myself to my husband. He is a gifted communicator and musician. He carries a lot of charisma and is very direct and passionate when he communicates. His way of communicating is quite different than mine. For some reason, I had this idea in my mind that all preachers and teachers were expected to be the same. *Successful teaching and preaching has to look a certain way, right?* So, when I would speak, I would get into a wrestling match with my own mind, thinking people would receive me better as a woman in ministry if I was more demonstrative like him. I couldn't be more wrong about that. When I finally stopped trying to be like him and decided to just be me, breakthrough happened in my life. It was an expectation I was putting on myself; people weren't putting that on me.

True freedom comes when you choose to be yourself. Ladies, when you speak, I encourage you to fully be you. You don't have to act like a man to bring forth a word of power and authority. When you're being true to yourself and living authentically, people will take notice and listen to what you have to say. *Authenticity* is your superpower.

How do you break free and overcome comparison? Here are a few different ways:

1. Write out declarations of what God says about you. The Bible is full of scriptures that speak to who you are. Here are a few examples:

    "Perhaps this is the moment for which you've been created" (Esther 4:14).

    "I praise you because I am fearfully and wonderfully made; your works are wonderful, I know that full well" (Psalm 139:14).

    "Do not fear. I have redeemed you. I have summoned you. You are mine" (Isaiah 43:1).

    "Do not be afraid or discouraged. For the Lord your God is with you wherever you go" (Joshua 1:9).

    "For I know the plans I have for you, declares the Lord, plans to prosper you and not to harm you, plans to give you hope and a future" (Jeremiah 29:11).

2. Practice gratitude. Start a gratitude journal. Take a few minutes each day to write down a few things you are grateful for. If it's hard to think of a few things, start with one for each day.

3. Learn how to celebrate others rather than secretly compete with them. If you're feeling intimidated by someone or find yourself comparing yourself to someone, ask yourself why. Then, find one thing about them that you see in yourself. Celebrate that thing you love about you rather than making the focus about them.

4. Learn to let the thing that is trying to create comparison become inspiration for you, and let it motivate you to be a better version of yourself in a healthy way.

5. Play the Glad Game and look for the good in yourself and others.

6. Love the Lord your God with all your heart, soul, mind, and strength and love your neighbor as you love yourself.

7. Learn to recognize and let go of limiting beliefs. You can't pour from an empty cup. If you are going to be who you are, you have to let go of the things holding you back, including ways of relating to others that keep the healthy you from emerging.

Why is it so important to break free in this area of your life?

What does comparison do to you? It keeps you second guessing yourself. And it often stirs up feelings of jealousy, envy and that you're not enough. It breeds a spirit of competition.

The key to breaking this spirit of comparison in our lives is to start believing and knowing that we truly are God's masterpiece created in His image. We say it all the time, but truly believing it is another story. In the space below, take a minute to write down some of the areas you have been struggling with when it comes to comparison.

A TIME OF
Reflection

Write down at least three areas where you have been struggling with comparison.

Now, write down three things that you love about yourself.

In what areas do you feel the most free?

"This Is Me"

_____

_____

_____

_____

_____

_____

_____

_____

_____

_____

DECLARATIONS

I am valuable and have purpose.

My life matters.

I have the strength to stand and be strong in the midst of difficult situations.

I am filled with the wisdom it takes to make good decisions.

In Christ, I am equipped with everything I need.

"TODAY YOU ARE YOU, THAT IS TRUER THAN TRUE. THERE IS NO ONE ALIVE WHO IS YOU-ER THAN YOU."

—DR. SEUSS

"NO ONE CAN MAKE YOU FEEL INFERIOR WITHOUT YOUR CONSENT."

—ELEANOR ROSEVELT

"COMPARISON IS THE THIEF OF JOY."

—THEODORE ROOSEVELT

"STOP COMPARING YOURSELF TO OTHER PEOPLE: YOU ARE AN ORIGINAL. WE ARE ALL DIFFERENT AND IT'S OKAY."

—JOYCE MEYER

GOD IS ALWAYS WITH US. EVEN

IN THE MIDST OF HARDSHIP.

EVEN WHEN OUR PLANS DON'T

GO AS EXPECTED.

99

09

God Remembers Your Dreams
Even if You Don't

'LL NEVER FORGET THE MOMENT I WAS sitting in the family room, waiting to hop online to chat with my husband Keith on Facebook Messenger. He had gone on a mission trip with our senior leader to the Fiji Islands, and I was excitedly waiting to hear from him. I sat quietly in my red rocking chair as the chat box opened. We chatted a few minutes, and then Keith popped a question on me. "How would you like to move our family to Fiji for the summer and start a ministry school there?"

At the time, we were in the middle of adopting a baby girl. Our kids had begged us for quite some time for a baby brother or sister, especially our son Micah. Years prior, we had medically removed the possibility of having another child of our own, so adoption was our only option. She was due to be born any day, and this was the reason I didn't go to Fiji with Keith.

So many questions went through my mind at that moment. *How would we move to Fiji with our two children and a third little baby? What would we do? Where would we live? What would we need to live in another country?* My mind was swirling, but my spirit was leaping inside. I told Keith that I was willing to do whatever God had in store for us, and the thought of that sounded like an amazing adventure. But first, we needed to pray and see if God was in it or if it was just a fun idea.

I remember getting off that call and feeling overwhelmed. I felt excited and scared. How would I manage a six-month-old baby, my other two children and launch a brand-new school in a nation I had never been to? I had no idea. As I was talking to Jesus about my fears and concerns, something really special happened.

The presence of God became very tangible and met me in the rickety, old red rocking chair I was sitting in. He reminded me of something I had said to Him when I was a young teenager.

You see, when I was about fourteen years old, the church I grew up attending hosted an annual mission conference. I loved sitting in the first or second row to catch all of the action. One year, they hosted the Fiji Choir, and while they were ministering in song, I remember asking the Lord if one day He would send me to their country. There was something about their culture that really resonated with me, and I knew I wanted to go there. I had an instant love toward the Fijian people and felt a special heart connection.

I had forgotten about that childhood dream, but God didn't. He knows the desires of our hearts and wants to give them to us, even the thoughts we've had in our youth. I sat there as the presence of God grew stronger, and I knew this was an assignment straight from God. I also knew that if He gives us an assignment, He will give us the grace we need to overcome everything needed to fulfill it.

He knows the desires of our hearts.

Keith made it home from Fiji, and then baby girl was born shortly after. We rushed to the hospital the night she was born, held her through the night, prayed over her and were ready to receive her as one of our own. After a long night, the birth mom decided she didn't want us to have her. At the time, we were all really sad because we had promises of having another child, and our kids really wanted another sibling. I even had several dreams about this little one that came true the moment she was born. We even had a name picked out that we believed the Lord gave us. How could we have missed hearing from God on this one? We felt we had a promise from God, but we also had to trust God in the midst of not seeing the promise fulfilled; God knew the bigger picture, and we couldn't see it yet. It reminds me of Abraham.

"Against all hope, Abraham in hope believed and so became the father of many nations, just as it had been said to him, 'So shall your offspring be.' Without weakening in his faith, he faced the fact that his body was as good as dead—since he was about a hundred years old—and that Sarah's womb was also dead. Yet he did not waver through unbelief regarding the promise of God, but was strengthened in his faith and gave glory to God, being fully persuaded that God had power to do what he had promised. This is why 'it was credited to him as righteousness'" (Romans 4: 18-22).

What do we do when we truly believe that we heard from God about a certain situation, and the outcome ends up different than we expected? What happens when we don't see promises fulfilled? What is the stance of our hearts? Do we keep standing and keep believing that God is good no matter what and that He sees the bigger picture? Or do we get mad at God and throw a fit? Do we stop trusting?

At times, I've done all of these things, as most of us do, but the important thing is to not allow ourselves to stay in that place of hopelessness and disappointment. Abraham believed and it was credited to him as righteousness. He was also written about in Hebrews 11 as being one of the great men of faith.

God sees so much more than we could ever think or imagine. Sometimes we think we know what's best for our lives and even try to make things happen in a certain way. We work really hard on a plan for our lives, thinking it's what's best for us, but then something changes and life goes in a different direction. Proverbs 16:9 says that in his heart a man plans his steps, but God directs the path of our hearts. God's ways are not our ways, but as we learn to trust, our faith gets stronger and beautiful things can happen.

> *As we learn to trust, our faith gets stronger and beautiful things can happen.*

Recently, I was at a store and a necklace stood out to me. It was a gold circle with a compass embossed on it. As soon as I saw it, I sensed the Holy Spirit speaking to me. "I am your true north. When hope is deferred for a season and things around you aren't looking good, always remember your inner compass is set to true north. I am with you always even to the ends of the earth."

God is always with us. Even in the midst of hardship. Even when our plans don't go as expected. We can find joy in the journey if our eyes are fixed on Jesus. He is the true author and perfecter of our faith.

As heartbroken as we were in the moment, God knew the season we were getting ready to step into. He also saw the bigger picture for that little girl's life. God had something else in mind for our family of four and her. Many things transpired since the day she was born, but now she is with the family that is a perfect fit for her.

Six months later, Keith, our nine-year-old daughter Maci, six-year-old son Micah, myself, and our dear friend Amanda boarded a jet plane and set out for Fiji. Little did we know that our entire family would have our lives changed forever. God remembered my childhood dream and had something special in mind for me and my family, just as He does for you.

A TIME OF
Reflection

What dreams have you had since you were a child?

Which of your dreams are you currently living?

Ask the Holy Spirit if there are any dreams you have forgotten about that He wants to remind you of today.

"You Know Me"

_____

_____

_____

_____

_____

_____

_____

_____

_____

DECLARATIONS

My dreams matter.

I am strong and courageous.

I pursue my dreams with the joyful expectation of good things coming my way.

God knows my future and He is for me.

GOD REMEMBERED MY
CHILDHOOD DREAM
AND HAD SOMETHING
SPECIAL IN MIND FOR ME
AND MY FAMILY, JUST AS
HE DOES FOR YOU.

99

DREAMS IGNITE PASSION

IN YOUR HEART. WHEN THIS

HAPPENS, HOPE BEGINS TO

RISE AND YOU START TO FEEL

ALIVE AGAIN.

99

10
Living the
Dream

WE ARRIVED IN FIJI – THE BEAUTIFUL COUNTRY I had dreamed about as a youth, and now there I was with my own children getting ready to step into a great God adventure.

We were instantly greeted with a warm Fijian hello, "bula vinaka," and a welcome home. After all these years my dream of spending time in Fiji was finally being fulfilled. However; Even though my heart and body were there in person, it was hard for me to wrap my head around the reality of this great adventure coming to pass. I still had a difficult time believing that God wanted me to step into and live my dreams. I had no idea how much my life was getting ready to change.

As a mom, there was no greater joy than to see our two children come fully alive when we were in Fiji. Our family made some pretty incredible memories together while we were there. We lived there for almost three months, and because we were launching a ministry school, people from the States would come to visit us almost weekly. This made our time even more special. My mom and sister even got to join us for a week.

We met so many beautiful people and got to experience Fijian Culture in such a special way. We planted a ministry school there, trained and equipped the Fijians how to hear from God at a greater level and release God's message of encouragement to others. We saw so many signs, wonders, and miracles. People were healed, delivered, set free and came to understand their Kingdom identity and value as a son and daughter of God. It was life changing, not only for them but for us. One of the values that we learned from our church leadership team in that season was something we all called strategic life exchange. Strategic life exchange means that everyone in a relationship has something of significant value to bring to the table. We all have things we can learn from one another. When we enter into relationships with this in mind it becomes a win-win situation and everyone learns and grows from their experience. Which is a beautiful thing.

After service one night, we were sitting having a meal together on the grass mats and my kids and I started praying for this young boy. We encouraged the children that were sitting with us to lay hands on and pray for him as well. He was deaf and mute. We prayed, and his ears and his voice opened up; he could hear and speak. All of his friends started shouting and cheering because he could repeat things we were saying, and they got to be a part of the miracle. It's something I'll never forget. Jesus healed him right there as we were all eating sandwiches and doing life together.

Both of our children had life-changing experiences while we were there. One day, we were driving through the town, and as we looked out the window, we all noticed things that were very different than our American culture. My son noticed how the young boys his age didn't have any shoes on. As a mom, I noticed that the sidewalks and streets had broken glass and garbage all over them. When we got back to the house, a group of boys was playing soccer in the field across from our house. The boys invited Micah to join them, so he kicked off his shoes and ran across the street. I shouted out, "Hey, Bud, you need your shoes to play soccer." He said, "No, Mom, I'm a Fijian now. I live in Fiji and

Fijians don't wear shoes." We all laughed and laughed in that moment. On special occasions I'd get Micah to wear his shoes.

Maci would walk around in public worshipping God and lifting her hands. I'd hear her singing new little songs that she would make up, and it really touched my heart. God met our entire family in that nation, and it will always hold a very special place in our hearts.

God knew I wasn't ready to step into my dream of visiting Fiji back when I was a teenager, but He planted a seed that night that would eventually become a reality for me. It took many years for that seed to take root and grow in my life, and God knew the exact elements and people that I would need to eventually connect with to see the dream come to fruition.

How many times has that happened to you? Have you ever gotten a creative idea or a prophetic word that says you'll be doing something specific and thought to yourself, *wow, that sounds amazing,* or *absolutely no way?* Maybe you've had a random thought which turns into another thought, and pretty soon those thoughts become the only thing you can dream about. All of a sudden, you have an entire plan on how you can make a lasting impact and change the world around you.

Dreams ignite passion in your heart. When this happens, hope begins to rise and you start to feel alive again. I've noticed a cycle with ideas and dreams. Sometimes the ideas come, and they are for you. Sometimes the ideas come and they are for someone else. When you get those ideas or words, it's always good to write them down so you can remember them. Take time to pray into them, and give yourself a little time to see if you are still excited about them a few weeks later. If you are, then take action and start testing them. If the initial excitement goes away, then maybe those things are for another season or for someone else.

However, when you feel it's time to take action on those dreams, you have to be willing to step out and take a risk. I call this the risk stage.

The risk stage is when you choose to move forward with something even if it doesn't work out the way you'd hoped. For your dreams to work, you must be willing to take many risks along the way.

Sometimes it takes years for things to come to pass. Oftentimes, it's either a timing issue or an obedience issue. However, as one of my mentors Dan McCollam says, *and I truly believe it,* "a person accelerates at the rate of their personal obedience."

I remember God giving Keith and I a promise: "You can have whatever house you want." When we heard this, I'm pretty sure we laughed just like Sarah and Abraham did when God told them they would have a baby in their old age. A home was the last thing we thought we could ever buy. We barely had enough money to put groceries on the table and were living on governmental aid at the time. However, this is something we had been dreaming about. It was a deep desire of ours to have a place we could call home.

You see, when we got married we moved to California to be youth pastors at a church. We were very excited to pursue the call of God on our lives no matter what the cost. Newly married, we ran a thriving youth group that was really growing and good things were happening. Our first apartment was a studio over a garage, and I remember being so excited to have a place of our own to start our lives together as husband and wife. It was perfect for just the two of us.

Little did we know that five months later, the senior leaders who brought us on staff would leave and we would be getting voted in as the next senior pastors of the church. We had just turned twenty-three years old.

I remember a phone conversation Keith and I had when we were dating, saying that if we ever moved to California, he thought he'd end up pastoring. I laughed back then to myself thinking *there is no way Keith will pastor his own church...maybe youth pastor, but not senior pastor.* Boy was I wrong. God had other plans. In less than a year's time, we had moved across the country, started youth pastoring and then became senior pastors of a church. We were excited, zealous and clueless about a lot of things, but we loved Jesus with all of our hearts.

This change opened up an opportunity for us to move across the street into the church parsonage. We didn't care. It was an upgrade from our little studio apartment. Now we'd have three bedrooms, two baths and a yard. The crazy thing is that the house we moved into was the *same exact house* Keith had grown up in. His parents had pastored the same church several years prior to us moving there.

The house was old, the walls were filled with mold, and it needed a lot of work. As time went on, we made a few changes as we lived there, but there were many more improvements that needed to be done.

We started having babies and started dreaming of entering a place of financial freedom and having our own space. We were able to stay in the house as part of our salary package which was great, but there came a time when we wanted to start building towards our future with a home of our own. We never saw this as more than a dream, but God started sending people to give us words about this becoming a reality.

Then, the promise came...*you can have whatever house you want.* Wow, was God going to just give us a house? If He said we could have whatever house we wanted, then that must be the case because we didn't have a dime to our name in savings for a down payment. But the promise propelled us forward in faith to pursue something that seemed impossible.

Keith and I started praying into that promise. We knew we needed to take action on it but didn't know what to do or even what house we

The promise propelled us forward in faith to pursue something that seemed impossible.

would want. We started driving around different areas in our community looking for houses and streets that we would enjoy living in. Anytime we found a place we would stop and pray. One day we found a house on a street that we liked and it had a for sale by owner sign in the front yard. We thought to ourselves... *could this be the one?*

For weeks we drove by the house. One day the owner was outside as we drove by, and Keith struck up a conversation with him. He told the guy we would like to have his house. Ha! God said we could have whatever house we wanted, right? That was the promise. The man invited us inside and showed us around. I couldn't believe it. He asked us several questions that day too, questions like, how do you plan on paying for a house? Were we pre-qualified? I don't even remember answering him. We were sitting there like two deer staring into this guy's headlights. He gave us a few pointers and said to come back when we had some answers and these things were complete.

These homeowners were so kind and told us a few helpful things to start us on a journey of purchasing our first home. We were two young kids with no clue on how to do all of this.

We left, and a few weeks later, we noticed the house had sold. We were devastated. It seems silly now looking back, but we really thought we were going to get that house. We had a promise from God! Little did we know we had a lot to learn.

After that day, we began to get things in order. We gathered the necessary paperwork and had conversations with our church board and others leaders in our lives. We started working with a real estate agent and found out how much we qualified for. It wasn't much, but at least we had something to work with.

After looking at several homes in our price range, we made an offer on a fixer upper located in a beautiful setting in the Redwoods. Our hopes were quickly deflated when we got the news that our offer wasn't accepted. This process was much more difficult than we thought. However, God knew we were not in a position to completely remodel a house that had been infested with mold and termites. I have no idea what we were thinking back then! All I know is we were eager to find a house to call home.

God was building our faith in this particular season. He wanted us to know His promise was true, and He was teaching us what it was like to hear His voice. I ended up having a dream about putting offers on houses, but we needed to offer the full asking price. He wanted us to keep pressing in. He wanted us to have our own place, but was also growing us up in the process. This process went on for many months.

I remember being away at worship school in Redding during the process of house hunting. I was there for six weeks and would come home during the weekends. It was a special time in my life where God was really calling me to Himself, and I was learning how to truly be His bride and growing in intimacy with Him. While learning to hear His voice, I was enjoying this new found relationship I had with Him.

As I sat out by the pool at the prayer house one day, I had a sweet encounter with the Lord. Acorns began to fall out of the tree, and it felt like somebody was throwing them at me to get my attention. It felt like someone was trying to say, "Hey, look at me! I want to get to know you." I took it as a sign from the Lord that He was drawing me closer and closer to Him. Our relationship was growing. I could feel it, and I just wanted to spend as much time alone with Him as I could. At the time, I was reading one of my favorite books called *The Bride*. It's an allegory by Rhonda Calhoun based on Song of Solomon in the Bible. It's an amazing book; I highly recommend it.

In the chapter I was reading that day, it was talking about the bridegroom preparing a home for his bride – a house made of cedar where deer and gazelle frolicked and played. The setting sounded so beautiful. I closed my eyes and imagined myself in that place. When I opened my eyes, three acorns were sitting right on the ground next to me. That seemed pretty significant, so I put them in my pocket and went on with my day.

Back at home that weekend, I was resting on the couch reading my book. I got to the part again where it said something about the bride being swept away by the bridegroom to a place made of cedar where deer and gazelles played. As I was finishing the chapter, Keith called out to me from the back room. "Hey, I think I found a house you're going to love. We should go look at it." He printed out the listing and brought it to me. Guess what the title of the listing was? "Custom Cedar Home Just for You," and the address was on Deer Road. *Wow, God, You truly are amazing and know every detail of our heart's desires.*

When I saw that, my hope for having a home was instantly renewed. I'd just had the encounter with the Lord while reading my book, saying, *God, I would love that kind of house.* So, we made an appointment with our agent to go see it. Within a few days we were writing up a full-price offer. Long story short and a few miracles later, God gave us what we needed to purchase our first home. A few months after that, we were living in this beautiful custom cedar home up in the California

Redwoods. That house became our first home. It was one of the most beautiful homes in our area, and it even had an indoor pool. It was the sweetest house, and it was a real blessing for us in that season.

Even though we didn't get the first house or the second one, God knew what was coming for us. His timing was perfect and things needed to shift in our hearts and our mindsets to even believe we could purchase a home. God was doing a work inside of us. He started the work by giving us a promise, but we had to follow through on a few things to *partner* with the promise we believed to be from God.

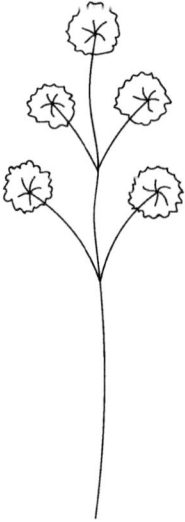

What are some things that you have been believing God for? Maybe it's to get out of debt or to purchase your very own home.

Ask God what promise He has for you.

One of the biggest lessons we learned from this experience is that when you get breakthrough in one area of your life, it's as if God gives you a new key to be able to access that place in the spirit whenever you need it. Faith that is built during the journey unlocks the freedom you need to access the dreams of your heart. The things we learned from buying our first home gave us the courage to pursue the next home, and even the next. We were able to access that place again because we learned how to pray, how to believe and how to take the needed action to partner with God to see those dreams become a reality.

A TIME OF
Reflection

What areas do you need faith in right now? What promise is God wanting to give you? Spend some time with God and ask Him to show you. Write down what you see or hear.

In what areas of your life do you feel God is asking you to step out and take a risk? Where do you need to take action to go to the next level in your life or relationships?

"Waymaker"

_____

_____

_____

_____

_____

_____

_____

_____

DECLARATIONS

God believes in my dreams.

My dreams are worthy of being pursued.

As I delight in Him, God will give me the desires of my heart

I have faith to believe for what seems impossible.

Breakthrough gives me access for more breakthrough.

FAITH THAT IS BUILT
DURING THE JOURNEY
UNLOCKS THE FREEDOM
YOU NEED TO ACCESS
THE DREAMS OF
YOUR HEART.

99

I REALLY BELIEVE THAT IF WE HAVE

EYES TO SEE AND EARS TO HEAR,

GOD WANTS TO SHOW US THINGS,

SPEAK THINGS TO OUR HEARTS

AND AWAKEN THINGS IN US THAT

HE WANTS TO BRING TO PASS IN

OUR LIFETIME THROUGH US.

99

11

Global Reform
Starts at Home

"If you want to change the world
go home and love your family."
—Mother Teresa

S O, WE DID. WE PULLED BACK FROM TRAVELING to make sure our priorities were in order. We knew our calling in God was great, however, our ministry to each other as husband and wife and to our children needed to come first. We could feel ourselves getting caught up in the whirlwind and excitement of world travel and ministry trips, and at times it was definitely an adrenaline rush. But the thought of losing our kids or each other in the midst of chasing our dreams in "ministry" and the nations anchored us to our core values, and we made the needed changes to course correct. Even though our kids would often go to the nations with us, it was getting to be too much for the season of life we were in. Our children needed us to be home, present and available to walk with them through life as teenagers.

Unfortunately, we have seen many others in ministry and life do this and lose their marriages or children in the process. Had we not course corrected, our story could have turned out much different.

During that season it felt like a circus act, trying desperately to keep all the plates spinning. You have to maintain incredible balance to do that well, and it felt like things were starting to spin out of control. I was simply doing too much and needed to pull back, even from some of the things I absolutely loved. The grace was starting to lift for me to work full time in the church, and once I recognized it was God lifting the grace from me it changed my perspective. He wanted to teach me something new and wanted to see if I was willing to listen and obey. Through the years, He's taught me how swift action and obedience often leads to acceleration or promotion. But even with the many lessons, I had a hard time letting go. Why? Probably because my identity was wrapped up in all of the things I did in church ministry. I've always been an overachiever. I enjoy doing things well and have a high standard for excellence, but God was trying to break the fear of man off of my life once and for all.

There's nothing wrong with doing things well and having a standard of excellence, but when you do things and *never* think you're doing a good job or you beat yourself up time and time again because you felt like you missed the mark, it isn't healthy. When you do this, you are holding yourself to a standard of performance rather than excellence.

As an artist, I understand. It's a vulnerable place to put something out there for anyone to see or hear, whether it be a piece of art, a song, a book, or something else creative. It's natural to want to be liked and receive affirmation. However, people have opinions and oftentimes aren't afraid to share them with you. Even as I write this book, I'm having to silence the voices and the scenarios my imagination makes up about all the negative things people might say about my journey. It's okay... everyone has the right to their opinions and they don't have to like what I create. But someone will, and that's who I am creating this for.

It's a vulnerable place to put something out there for anyone to see or hear.

Not everyone will like you, even if you are the kindest, most amazing person on the planet. Everyone has their stories, and not all stories are good. The amazing thing is that even in the midst of a bad story, if we choose to let God into it, He will give us beauty for ashes and joy for our journey.

Tired of spinning the plates, I grabbed my journal to process with the Lord. As an internal processor, it's really helpful for me to write out my thoughts and prayers. I'll process out my thoughts, turn them to prayers, wait for the Lord to speak to me and then write those words down.

God already knew all that was going on with church life behind the scenes. He didn't need me to tell Him, but He welcomed my tear-lined journal pages filled with ink and mascara.

There was so much going on that my heart was aching. I was crying for days. I was tired. Our church youth group had suffered an unspeakable loss and were going through a massive transition that affected many families, including our own. *How, God? Why, God?* I didn't get it. I had all the questions and zero answers. All I knew was to hold onto God with every ounce of hope I could muster. I'd find scriptures in the Bible on the topic of hope, but not much brought me comfort. I'd go to church and see the look in these young people's eyes, and it would break my heart. They, too, had lost hope. *Would any of us recover?*

Thankfully, my husband Keith was able to step in and help serve those young people, but it wasn't easy. God knew what they were going to need by positioning my husband to help with the youth. I watched his heart grow for youth exponentially in that season, and it literally has changed the lens by which we see God's heart for all generations. He loves the old and the young just the same. Not only does He love them, but He sees them.

As I mentioned before, my mama's heart had a hard time dealing with all the things. During a heart to heart with Jesus one morning, I heard Him ask me the very thing I ask others: "If time or money wasn't an issue for you, what would you be doing right now?" I thought to myself, *Lord, is this a trick question? You know I love the nations and would love to travel, but the season we are in right now is not even an option for that.* I knew that wasn't what He was talking about...He wanted me to get out of my head and dream outside of the box.

I wasn't really in a big dreaming place then. Honestly, I didn't want to do or add anything else. My plate was already full with serving on our core leadership team, worship director/leader, children's ministry overseer, wife, and mom, and occasionally I'd get a job outside the church to help supplement our income. It was a lot, and the grace was lifting. But He asked me again, "If time or money wasn't an issue, what would you be doing?"

*Okay, well...*I sat there, and in that moment the only thing I could think of was *I'd like to do hair.* I'd always had a knack for doing hair, but I wanted to do it professionally and make money doing it.

That's what I said, very matter-of-factly. I was kind of being bratty about it because I had always regretted not going to beauty school right out of high school. Now I was in my early forties and didn't really think it was going to be an option anymore. So, I wrote about it in my journal and prayed about it for several weeks. My prayer was *God, You know I would like to go to beauty school. However, if this is some random pipe dream and it doesn't fit into my destiny, then please take the desire away from me.*

As I prayed about it, the desire got stronger and stronger; it was not lifting, and honestly it was making me a little bit frustrated. You see, I had tried to go to beauty school at least two other times during my married life and didn't have the greenlight to go forward, so I never did. Now I was at a different type of crossroads, and God was asking me the time or money question. Little did I know that this question would set me on a different course for a completely new season of our lives.

Has God ever spoken something to you or asked you a question that made you wonder *God, is this really You? Do You want me to do something different that I've never done before? Do You actually care about the dreams and desires in my heart, even the ones I might've tucked away as a little girl? The ones You and I talked about when nobody else was listening? The ones I've only shared with You?*

Oftentimes our tendency is to hold on to things we need to let go of. Imagine holding an object in your hand. If you hold on to the object so tightly and someone walks by and wants to put something new in your hand, you won't be able to grab onto the new thing. However, if you hold an object loosely in your hand, then you can let go of what needs to go and at the same time receive something new. Holding things loosely creates space to hold onto both.

I really believe that if we have eyes to see and ears to hear, God wants to show us things, speak things to our hearts and awaken things in us that He wants to bring to pass in our lifetime through us. All He needs is our yes; when He has our yes, anything can happen. I've seen it time and time again. I've seen God come through miraculously and provide in ways that blows my mind.

A TIME OF
Reflection

Are there any areas in your life where you know you need to let go? If so, what are they? Where have you been spinning all of the plates in your life?

Ask God to show you if there is something new He wants to give you or do in you?

Have you been holding yourself to a standard of performance rather than excellence? What is God showing you about that?

"Take Courage"

DECLARATIONS

God, You have my yes.

My yes to God and my family is more important than anything else.

God cares about the dreams in my heart.

I'VE SEEN GOD COME
THROUGH MIRACULOUSLY
AND PROVIDE IN WAYS
THAT BLOWS MY MIND.

99

IF WE GO THROUGH THE HARD

TIMES WITH HIM, THEN WE'RE

CERTAINLY GOING TO GO

THROUGH THE GOOD TIMES

WITH HIM!

99

12
The Glad Game

I REMEMBER A TIME WHEN I WAS REALLY struggling with someone close to me. They said some things that really hurt my heart right before I was getting ready to speak at a church. Keith and I had traveled to minister together, and my phone rang on the way to the meeting. Of course, I answered it, and then that conversation left me feeling very upset to the point of tears.

Their words came out like daggers piercing my heart. Through the years, I had learned how to deal with this, because this type of behavior was normal for this particular person, but that day it caught me completely off guard and made me angry. I couldn't find the right words to speak during the conversation and felt in that moment it was best to not say anything in response. I was upset to the point of not being able to think straight, so how in the world was I going to get up and preach?

During worship, I tried to redirect my focus and get into a sweet spot. I prayed, tried to forgive that person, repented for being angry, etc., but the aggravation would not leave. I was so irritated. I was sitting quietly in a puddle of my own tears when I heard the Holy Spirit speak to me, "I want you to make a list of ten things you like about this person that hurt you." *Ugh, Lord, why? I can't even think of one thing.* Of course, there were several amazing things, but in that moment I was at a loss.

Nothing came to mind. Then, in my mind's eye, I saw this person cooking a meal. *Fine*, I thought, *that's what I'm going to write down.*

He's great at making _____.

And then, I was stuck again. *Lord, why do I have to do this? What's the big deal? I don't get it; I just want to feel better and peaceful again.* He said, "Then you'd better start writing. What else is he good at?" I could feel a lesson was about to be learned. So, I started writing. I literally made a list of the next few things...

He's good at _____.

He's good at_____.

Ugh. God, this is frustrating, nothing else is coming to mind. Please help me love this person and see him the way You see him. The next few things came to mind.

He did this for me _____.

He's really creative.

He can do this _____.

After writing a few more things down, the heaviness started to lift. After every good thing I wrote down, I started feeling lighter and lighter. *Okay, God, I'm starting to get it. When I choose to forgive, and then focus on the good and not the bad, atmospheres change.* My heart starts to change. Forgiveness became my reality, and goodness brought my attitude up.

Forgiveness and goodness are keys to unlocking freedom in people's hearts. I needed to understand this lesson at a greater level personally, but also because He wanted to bring freedom in the meeting we were getting ready to speak in. Forgiveness and focusing on the good were the keys needed for the night – for me and everyone there. I was starting to catch the lesson. I wrote a few more things:

He's amazing at _____.
Great at _____.
Really good at _____.
Wow, _____ is actually pretty amazing.

My attitude shifted. My heart changed, and God was able to use my story to bring freedom and change history for people that night. Lives were touched. People were able to forgive people who had hurt them years ago, and souls were saved.

There are so many things to be thankful for if we choose to see the good around us. I am not denying that sometimes things are really tough. I've walked through my share of tough and seriously devastating situations and life circumstances. However, when you learn the art of seeing life as the cup being "half full" rather than half empty, your perspective changes, which makes a huge difference. At the end of the day, it's up to us. Being positive is a choice.

One of my favorite movies is an older Disney movie called *Pollyanna*. It's a story of a little girl who lived in a very negative world; everyone around her was extremely negative and processed life through the lens of negativity. Pollyanna was full of life and joy, and people around her were always trying to dull her sparkle. For a while they did, until one day she decided to play a game that would forever change the course of life – for her and those around her.

Her game was called The Glad Game. Pollyanna learned to take the negative and flip it into a positive. She was on a mission to find and see the good in life, so when someone would say something bad about someone, she'd find a way to bring out the good. It was like she was on a constant treasure hunt, calling out the good in people's lives. As she played her game, people began to take notice and shift happened. Life began to spring forth and lives were drastically changed.

There's something all of us can learn from the life of this little girl. Perspective is everything; how we see life and interpret it is a really big deal. Maybe you're saying to yourself after reading this, *Heather, you have no clue. You don't know the pain of what I've walked through. No one understands me, no one sees me, so how could things ever change for me?* If you're saying these things to yourself, it's time for an upgrade in your thinking, there is a better way.

Are you tired of being sad or even depressed at times? Have you hit the bottom more times than you can count? Do you struggle with seeing the good in anything? I invite you to play The Glad Game with me. For the next 21 days, let's make a choice to intentionally choose life and play The Glad Game. Make it a point to see the good in yourself and in others around you.

Here are a few ideas to get you started.

Choose to look for the good. Go on a treasure hunt looking for the good around you. Treasure isn't the easiest to find. You must search for it, and sometimes it takes a while to find, but when you do you find incredible wealth.

Go on a treasure hunt looking for the good around you.

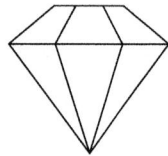

Turn a negative situation into a positive one. If someone is being negative, rather than agreeing with them, find a way to share something positive and redirect the focus to that regardless of how ugly the situation might be.

Think happy thoughts. If your mind is racing around a negative track, make it stop by thinking of something that personally makes you happy. Let your mind and heart hang there for a while.

Don't give up! If you're having a hard time with the challenge, it's okay. You are perfectly normal. It takes 21 days to break old habits and establish new patterns of thinking,

Practice speaking life over yourself. Write down ten things you love about yourself and post them somewhere you look often. Transformation has to start with you first, and it will help you see the good in others

Have fun! Life is meant to be an exciting adventure with God. I love what The Message Bible says about this in Romans 8:14-17.

> "God's Spirit beckons. There are things to do and places to go! This resurrection life you received from God is not a timid, grave-tending life. It's adventurously expectant, greeting God with a childlike 'What's next, Papa?'"

God's Spirit touches our spirits and confirms who we really are. We know who He is, and we know who we are: Father and children. And we know we are going to get what's coming to us – an unbelievable inheritance! We go through exactly what Christ goes through. If we go through the hard times with Him, then we're certainly going to go through the good times with Him!

A TIME OF
Reflection

Ask God if there is anyone you need to forgive. Ask God to help you see the good in that person.

Make a list of ten things you like and appreciate about that person.

Pray and release them to God.

"The Glad Game Video"

_____

_____

_____

_____

_____

_____

_____

_____

_____

DECLARATIONS

As I fix my eyes on Jesus my eyes can see and pull out the good in others.

The Glad Game is my secret weapon.

Forgiveness and goodness are my keys to unlocking freedom in people's hearts.

I choose to walk in joy and release Hope to others.

GOD'S SPIRIT TOUCHES
OUR SPIRITS AND
CONFIRMS WHO WE
REALLY ARE. WE KNOW
WHO HE IS, AND WE
KNOW WHO WE ARE:
FATHER AND CHILDREN.

99

WHEN YOU ARE PURSUING THE

DREAMS OF YOUR HEART,

IT REQUIRES YOU

TO TAKE ACTION.

99

13
Pursuing
Your Dreams

GROWING UP, I HAD MANY DREAMS. I wanted to go away to college, get married and have two children. I dreamt of the home I would have and filling it with beautiful things to make a cozy, rest-filled, loving, peaceful place for my children to grow up and be nurtured. I dreamt of places I wanted to take my family. I also dreamt of being in ministry alongside my husband, traveling and ministering all around the world where we could share the love, freedom and kindness of Christ with others.

My dreams included living in other countries. I dreamt of having lifelong friends who know me and love me. I dreamt of having a family who was completely in love with Jesus and lived their lives completely sold out for Him. I dreamt of writing songs, singing on stage and even producing a CD. I would create beautiful art that would be sellable. I dreamt of going to other countries to help create sustainable projects that would generate income and transform people's lives. I dreamt of taking teams around the world to love on the poor and broken, treating them like they are royalty, clothing them, feeding them, honoring them in their lives and celebrating the beautiful people they are.

Almost every one of these things I dreamt about have become a part of my story. But something in my heart really wanted to go back to school to do hair. It was the one thing I regretted not doing right after high school. But it never seemed to be the right time for me...until it was.

When I was working full time in the church and the grace for doing church ministry full time was starting to lift, God was shifting the season for both my husband and me. It felt very uncomfortable because working in the church environment had been our life for over twenty years. There were seasons when I would work outside the church, but the majority of my time was spent working in church culture.

One day, I remember journaling while having quiet time with the Lord. I was writing out my dreams and desires, but also venting my frustrations and putting them on paper. Journaling or doing something creative is one of the ways I like to process my thoughts, feelings and emotions. I naturally process things internally. I don't enjoy talking about things out loud until I mull it over in my mind or heart for a while first. This internal dialogue process helps me come to a conclusion on what I want to say, I am an internal processor. On the other hand, external processors tend to talk about things out loud and even say things that may not be correct, but by doing so will come to a conclusion and or solution by themselves. My husband and I joke about this because he externally processes everything, and I'm the complete opposite.

Through the years, we've learned that this can create conflict in relationships unless you learn the art of doing the internal/external dance. One thing that has helped us in our marriage with communication is that whenever we have a deep conversation, I ask if he is just needing me to listen or wanting input. For years, I would offer advice when he was sharing something he was processing. I thought I was helping the situation, but I was actually doing the opposite. And he was the same with me. I would share, and he would offer advice when I wasn't wanting or asking for it, so we'd both leave the conversation upset or frustrated.

What does this have to do with dreams in your heart becoming a reality? A lot actually, especially if you are married. It's important to be real and honest with yourself and your closest relationships. If you are not honest it can be detrimental to your relationships and your heart.

As I was sitting there journaling and processing, I heard the Lord ask me the time or money question I mentioned earlier. I sat quietly and answered.

Later that afternoon, I was out running errands and decided to stop by the local beauty school in our city. I went inside and asked if I could set up a tour, and the admissions lady said, "Sure, do you have time right now?" We proceeded to walk around and tour the campus. The rooms were full of young men and women learning hair, makeup, massage, etc. They were all laughing and enjoying one another. As we left the makeup room, I found myself with tears streaming down my face. I kept wiping my eyes, not wanting her to see me crying. For some reason I couldn't help it; the tears wouldn't stop.

After the tour, we went into the office and she handed me a packet full of information with the financial investment, dates, scholarship opportunities, and more. I got back to my car, took one look at the price and my heart sank. We were in no position to be able to afford this school at this point in our lives, and we had made a commitment to not go into financial debt anymore. I remember hitting my steering wheel with my packet of information and crying out, "God! Why do I have this desire if I'm never going to be able to go? If I can't go, please take this desire away." Immediately, I heard (almost audibly),

"Why can't you?"

Have you ever wanted to do something so bad but the timing was off? God cares about the desires of your heart. He sees the things that you care about. He sees your silent tears. He knows your desires. And He also sees the big picture of how *all* things work together for good for those who love Him and are called according to His purposes (Romans 8:28). His timing is perfect even when we don't think it is.

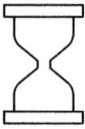

Timing requires trust.

I was shocked when I heard the words *why can't you.* I had been so used to hearing the word no about going to beauty school. Mentors even told me years prior that they didn't see how this would fit into my life, but it was something I just couldn't shake. I knew this was the Lord speaking to me.

What do you mean why can't you? Was I finally getting a green light? Was God telling me that I could finally do this and the timing was right? Peace filled my heart in an instant, and I went straight home to share my afternoon adventure with Keith. I wasn't expecting him to be on board, but I knew I could trust that it would work out if God was in this.

When I got home, his response was just as I had imagined. "Woman! You're crazy." Ha! Well, he may not have said those *exact* words, but that is exactly what he was thinking. Remember earlier when I said he says things out loud sometimes? Yeah, this was one of those moments. We had to talk through all of our thoughts and concerns, come up with a plan, and then pray about how we'd come up with the money. Our conclusion was that if God was in it, He'd help us come up with the finances to fund the dream.

As I was looking through the packet one day, I noticed several scholarship opportunities were available, but there was only one that paid up to half of your tuition. The admissions officer made it a point to share the opportunities with me on my initial visit, but also made mention that she'd never seen anyone win any of the scholarships available in the entirety of her working for the program. That wasn't super encouraging, but I knew I wanted to at least try for one of them. Remember, I had no money and needed to figure out a way to pay for this dream of twenty plus years.

I looked for the highest paying scholarship on the list and decided that was the one I would work to pursue. And that's exactly what I did. When I read the lengthy requirements, fear tried to grip me again. There were so many things on that list that I needed to do. Feeling the fear again made me mad, but on the other hand it made me fight. It made me fight for my freedom and fight to hold the ground I had already taken in the realm of fear.

When we are taking new ground, the enemy wants us to fail. He wants to inhibit us from walking in freedom. His number one plan is to steal, kill and destroy our lives, but we have to remember that God came to give us life – not just a regular average life, but an abundant life. We see this in John 10:10.

One of the requirements was to make a three-minute video of what I wanted to "Shout Through Beauty." When I read that I needed to film a video, I tangibly began to feel fear. My mind went blank. *What would I do? How would any of this come together?* I didn't know, but what I did know was that I had faith to see this through, and I knew how to pray. I wanted to win this scholarship so badly. I wanted this breakthrough for not only me, but my family too. I wanted to be an example to my teens that it was okay to pursue the dreams of your heart and take risks even when it seems impossible.

God wants to give us the desires of our heart as we delight in Him. Psalm 37:4 says that if we delight ourselves in the Lord, He will give us the desires of our heart. This is one of my favorite scriptures. I've seen it come true in my own life time and time again. This was a promise I knew I had to hold onto to press through the fear and be courageous.

When you are pursuing the dreams of your heart, it requires you to take action. Most of the time it's not easy. There were requirements that needed to be fulfilled if I wanted to win that scholarship contest. I actually had to do something and get creative. Oftentimes, we are not willing to do the hard work required to see our dreams become a reality. It wasn't going to happen by me *thinking happy thoughts, praying great prayers,* or by *wishing.* All of those are great things, but they alone won't get anything done. I wanted to go back to school but didn't have the money.

Faith requires action.

Going back to school was only the beginning of pressing into this dream. More would come later, but this was the first step. I saw an opportunity, took a risk, had faith that God would meet me in my place of desire and weakness and jumped head first into the unknown. Hundreds of applicants from all over the United States applied for this scholarship, and only ten applicants would win.

In faith and agreement with my family, I applied for the school and started working on the scholarship video. I needed to know if this beauty school dream was real or just a pipe dream. I truly believe that all dreams need to be tested so we can come to that conclusion. I'll talk more about how to do that in another chapter.

I spent an afternoon hanging out with the Lord and praying about what I could put in my video. I wanted to share my story. I wanted to communicate God's heart through my story, even through a scholarship video. My prayer in life is that whatever I do, I want it to be a blessing to God and to others. I needed creative God ideas and an action plan to do this well.

When I'm working on projects or trying to get ideas for things, I like to ask myself the following questions:

Why do I want to do this?
Who is the main audience I will be sharing this with?
How can I use this to make an impact on those around me?
What is the message I want to communicate?
Is there a theme?
What are the elements needed to complete this project?
When is this supposed to be completed?

Answering these things gives me understanding and courage to know there is purpose to my pursuit.

That day, I wrote a script for my video and started putting a team together to help me execute the ideas I put on paper.

Dreams take action for them to become a reality. I think this is where people miss it. Many people have a dream or an idea in their heart that they think will just magically appear or drop in their lap without them doing anything about it.

Years ago, I remember meeting with a prophetic leader and mentor. I was sharing some dreams in my heart but was having a challenging time communicating them. He said, "Heather, you need to write down your dreams so you can get clarity of your vision. Organize your ideas on paper. Write them down in such a way that you could hand the paper to anyone and they would have everything they needed to execute what they were reading." This was a huge revelation for me. For years I thought dreams were just something you would think about in your mind or things you'd have when you were sleeping. It wasn't until I met with that leader that I gained insight into how to follow through with a heart dream to see it come to reality.

If we don't take action on our dreams, they are either just good ideas or they fit into the pipe-dream category. Pipe dreams are the dreams we tend to glamorize in our minds. They are the ones we think will give us the affirmation or recognition we long for. The ones we think are amazing ideas because we see them going well for someone else. If we do the exact same thing as they do, we will get the exact same result, right? Sometimes that works, and sometimes it doesn't. Most of the time it's not even within our grace or gift set but is just a glorified wish or idea. These types of dreams usually don't end well. True freedom comes when your heart dreams, heart strings and calling come into alignment.

After lots of dreaming, hoping, planning and preparing, I along with a few of my dear friends put together a winning video. (It's on YouTube if you'd like to see it). Out of hundreds of applicants, I was one of the ten scholarship winners, and they told me my video came out on top. With God's help, I graduated with top honors as the class valedictorian and got to speak at graduation. I knew this journey would be the beginning of new adventures with God; it would open up a new realm of possibilities in the Kingdom.

"

True freedom comes when your heart dreams, heart strings and calling come into alignment.

"

A TIME OF
Reflection

How do you process information? Are you an internal or an external processor?

As you read this chapter, does anything come to mind that you may have been putting off, something God is bringing back to the surface? Do you have heart dreams that you need to re-visit?

"Come Alive Dry Bones"

Take a few moments and journal your thoughts. Ask God what He thinks about what you are feeling. Write those thoughts down.

DECLARATIONS

My dreams matter.

God has placed dreams in my heart, and He wants to help me with them.

God's timing is perfect.

IF WE DON'T TAKE ACTION
ON OUR DREAMS, THEY
ARE EITHER JUST GOOD
IDEAS OR THEY FIT
INTO THE PIPE-DREAM
CATEGORY.

SOMETIMES WE HAVE TO

OVERCOME THE FEAR OF BEING

SEEN OR BEING SUCCESSFUL

TO STEP INTO THE FULLNESS OF

WHAT GOD IS CALLING US INTO.

99

14

Testing Your
Dreams

DREAMS AND DESIRES OF YOUR HEART need to be tested. In the last chapter, I mentioned that true freedom comes when three things come into alignment: heart dreams, heart strings and your calling.

As I was graduating from beauty school, a dear family friend sent me a video link. He said, "Hey, I think you might be interested in this." I watched the video, and the tears started to flow. It was a story of an artist in the beauty industry who wanted to bring change to her family and others. She created a hair extension method that quickly became a sought-after luxury brand. People paid her thousands of dollars to have their hair done with this method and treated it more as an investment in their self-care routine. One of the things I had decided, as I was getting ready to graduate and dive into the beauty industry, was that I wanted to find out what the highest-paying service was in a salon and specialize in that. When I watched the video, I knew this would be my pathway forward.

Even though I was a new artist in the industry, the Lord had been taking me on a journey of understanding my value. I knew from the start I didn't want to slave behind the chair making $10 an hour and working eight to ten-hour days. I wanted more than that, so I was willing to do whatever it took to get to that place.

At the end of the video, there was a link to sign up for the training that this artist was offering. It was $1000 to attend the event and get certified. The training was a three-day event in Southern California at an expensive resort hotel in Huntington Beach. That meant I would also need to purchase airfare and three nights at a hotel. We were still in quite a financial crunch during that season. Keith and I talked it through and decided it was a good investment.

After attending the event and getting certified, we were invited to apply for an advanced certification course that was even a higher ticket price. The price made my jaw drop, but we were in a season of breaking a poverty spirit, so I knew I needed to figure out how I could make this happen. I applied, did the work needed to get accepted and dove deeper into the rabbit hole. Three years later, I was recognized as one of the first twenty-five licensed artists within the brand globally. For me this was a very high honor.

The pursuit of this dream in the beauty industry was filled with purpose and passion, and God's hand was all over it. It was clear through some of the outcomes, that I was on the right track with God in this journey. Unfortunately, many of us never find out if God is in something because we are not willing to step out to test the dream. That's one thing I've learned to do: test my dreams.

Here are a few things you can ask yourself as you think of testing and pursuing your dreams.

Ask yourself: If time or money were not an issue, what would I be doing?

Give yourself time to really think about this question, then start making a list. Allow yourself to dream big here. If it's difficult to dream big, start with the first things that come to mind, and then write them down. As you begin to write, more things will come to mind. You can always go back later and refine your list; in fact, you definitely will need to. But let yourself dream with the same sense that Walt Disney had when he said, "If you can dream it, you can do it."

I've never let time or money hold me back from pursuing my dreams. I know that I will always be stretched in the pursuit of dreams, and at times it is very uncomfortable. Even so, I know that through the process, much growth will happen, and I will become a better version of myself. Taking that advanced course in the beauty industry was a huge risk for me, but the growth was exponential. It was just the test I needed to see if this dream would really become a passion of mine. I came out of that journey knowing I was on the right track with God.

Sometimes you have to say no to things to be able to say yes to the dream you're supposed to pursue.

Ask yourself: Are there things in my life I need to start saying no to, in order to say yes to my dreams?

If so, make another list of what those things are. It's okay to start saying no. In fact, you'll have to become really good at saying the word no in order to focus on the things you need to say yes to. Trust me, it's not easy if you are good at saying yes to everything in order to please others. Saying no is a good starting point and a great boundary to put into place. You will find that saying no will bring you peace. It's a really good thing, I promise. It doesn't always feel great to say no, but when you start seeing the results of your dream taking shape, it will be worth it.

Ask yourself: What is working in my life, and what is not working?

Be brutally honest and make yourself another list. If you have to, share that list with someone who knows you very well, someone like a spouse, a family member, or a friend. Then, ask them if you were being honest. They will tell you.

Take action: Look at your list. What are some things you can begin doing now that line up with what you wrote down?

Don't be afraid to start small. It's really important to test your dreams and ideas, and it's okay to try something to see if it's really for you or not. If you have big dreams about living in another country but you've never even left the country or city that you live in, it's time to take a trip. Do you have a passport? If not, you'd need to get one. Do you know anything about that place? Have you done any research on the people or the culture? Have you done what it takes to get you started in the right direction?

There will always be some first steps to seeing your dreams take shape, so you have to be willing to answer these questions and take the baby steps. If you don't, you'll never move forward with the bigger things. It's so important to be faithful with the small things like we see in Matthew 25:21.

> "His master said to him, 'Well done, good and faithful servant. You have been faithful over a little; I will set you over much. Enter into the joy of your master.'"

For dreams to work, you have to BELIEVE.

"If you can believe, all things are possible to him who believes" (Mark 9:23). You have to believe in yourself and believe in your dream. It's in your heart for a reason. Ask yourself the following questions:

1. What are the things that make me come alive?

2. Why does it make me come alive?

When you find that thing (what) and that reason (why), it will propel you forward, making what's in your heart become a reality.

Another important thing is to make sure you keep your vision in front of you. I like to start doing this by praying into it. If I want to do something, I lather it in prayer. If I want to go somewhere or start a project, I'll pray into it. I put pictures together of people's faces. I start wrapping my heart around the thing that's stirring in my heart. I'll put a vision and prayer board together by cutting out photos or words from magazines that have special meaning to me around a specific dream or theme, and then glue it all together in one place. I'll put thoughts and prophetic words that God has said about it together on the same board. When it's done, I put it somewhere I can see it to keep it in front of me, even when I'm not thinking about it.

For example, have you ever wanted to lose weight and put a photo of yourself on your mirror or fridge as a reminder of what your goal is? Maybe it's a picture of what you want to look like, or maybe it's a picture of what you don't want to look like...same concept. Create something visual that will help keep your vision in front of you. Then, set some goals for yourself and track your progress. Where do you want to be in a week? In a month? In three months? This time next year? Write it all down.

For years, I've heard my husband's and my mentor Dan McCollam share about dreams and how to test the dreams in your heart. This way of thinking has now become a way of life for my husband and me. When we are at any major crossroad or are making any major decision, we always take the following things into consideration. Dan always said to pay attention to these three things:

1. What areas are you passionate about? What are the things that you're constantly thinking about? What are you really good at?

2. What are your burdens? What are the things that pull on your heart strings? What are the things that bring you to tears? What are the things that make you angry and bring about a sense of injustice?

3. What do you feel called to? What are you naturally gifted at? In which areas of your life do you have massive favor or influence? These can be the things or opportunities that seem to present themselves to you on a regular basis.

After you answer these things, take note of the history of your life. What jobs and experiences have you had? Are there commonalities? How do they all work together? For me, I've found that there has been a definite thread of passion throughout my entire life. Let me give you an example.

Ever since I was young, I've had a love for music. I started singing when I was in fourth grade. Art and music were required classes while I was growing up, which I am so grateful for because that has changed over the years. In junior high and high school, I was in multiple choirs, including All State Choir and the church's worship team. This love of singing continued into my college years where I met my husband Keith in our college's traveling singing group. We quickly fell in love, got married and even began singing together on occasion. As I grew in confidence, I began leading worship for church and large conferences and events. The thread of music has run through my entire life.

Some of us have one thread, and some of us may have many threads. When you find the commonalities, it helps you see the areas of passion in your life, and this plays a huge factor in your purpose.

When we delight ourselves in the Lord by spending time with Him and keep Him as the center of our lives while doing things we love, the desires of our heart naturally come to fruition. This is one of God's promises found in Psalm 37:4: "Delight yourself in the Lord and he will give you the desires of your heart."

When these common threads of life come together, it will help you understand how you are wired and what makes you come alive. Over the next several pages, I want you to take some time to answer some questions. It's okay if you don't have all the answers immediately. Remember, this is just the beginning. Start with a simple idea or thought. Do some brainstorming. Without a plan, the gift of freedom you have for yourself and others can never become a reality. Sometimes we have to overcome the fear of being seen or being successful to step into the fullness of what God is calling us into.

A TIME OF
Reflection

Passions: What areas of life are you passionate about? What are the things that you're constantly thinking about? What are you really good at?

Burdens: What are your burdens? What are the things that pull on your heart strings? What are the things that bring you to tears? What things make you angry and bring about a sense of injustice?

"Come Alive"

Giftings or Experience: What do you feel called to? Which areas are you naturally gifted at? Which areas of your life do you have massive favor or influence? These can be things or opportunities that seem to present themselves to you on a regular basis.

....

....

....

....

....

....

....

DECLARATIONS

I am passionate about _____.

Being courageous and taking risks will accelerate the ability for my dreams to become a reality.

I have what it takes to see the things in my heart come to pass.

I am confident that He who began a good work in me will carry it on to completion.

DELIGHT YOURSELF IN
THE LORD AND HE WILL
GIVE YOU THE DESIRES
OF YOUR HEART.

99

?

WHEN GRACE STARTS TO LIFT

FOR SOMETHING, YOU HAVE TO

START ASKING YOURSELF

A FEW HARD QUESTIONS.

99

15
Step Into a
New Day

THE TIDE WAS TURNING FOR ME AND MY FAMILY. Change was inevitable, as our season in Northern California was coming to an end. We had a pretty strong word about five years prior that when our son graduated from High School, it would mark a season shift for our family. That time had come, and we were seeking God about where He would be calling us next.

Our best friends had moved down to Southern California and invited us to come down and visit. Keith went down there for a few days to check things out and came back very excited. He absolutely loved it. He loved Orange County, he loved the beach, he loved the fact that our friends lived there and all the things were lining up for him...but I couldn't quite see it. Honestly, I don't think I wanted to see it. I knew it was time for change, but I also had a good group of established friends and family close by, plus I was gaining momentum in my hair extension business. The idea of leaving it all behind made me sad.

We came to an agreement: we would take the family down for a week toward the end of June and see what everyone thought. I don't think any of us would ever say no to a beach vacation, so we booked our hotel, hopped in the car and drove down to meet up with our friends in Huntington Beach. The plan was to spend time there, scope out the area and see if it had potential for us to move there as well.

The hair extension salon that I had been connected to and training with for the past few years was also in Orange County; I wanted to experience being a client there, so I made a hair appointment while we were on vacation. As I was driving to the salon, I stopped at a stoplight on the Pacific Coast Highway, and my GPS starting making noise. Siri kept telling me to turn right. I knew the way to the salon was straight, so I was a little perplexed at Siri's persistence. Momentarily, I'd need to make a quick decision on which way to go. Right then, a huge, orange monarch butterfly appeared and flew right in front of my windshield and over to my driver's window. Because butterflies have always been either a sign to me that God is trying to tell me something or that breakthrough is here, I took note of it. There have been many stories throughout my life where this has proven to be true, so because of the butterfly, I made the decision to turn right.

As I drove down this backstreet, I began to fall in love with the area that Siri and the orange butterfly had guided me to. It was beautiful and the homes were incredible. I would have loved to spend more time there exploring, but I couldn't be late for my appointment. As I was sitting at another stoplight getting ready to turn right back onto the main highway, a song came on the radio. Immediately God's presence filled the car, and I'll never forget the song's words: step into a new day. I had never heard this song before, but as I continued to listen, I felt that God was speaking to me. Tears started to stream down my face.

As soon as the song was over, another popular song came on called "The Blessing." Again, tears started streaming down my face. This song also had tremendous meaning to me. I had a vision of our senior leader singing this song over us and praying over us like it was our final service at the church we had been serving at for the past twelve years. Right then, I knew God was telling me it was time to start a new chapter, and it was okay to leave Vacaville. When I arrived at the salon, I grabbed my phone and texted Keith immediately, "Hi, Love, I got the breakthrough I needed. God spoke to me and I'm okay with moving to Southern California." Two weeks later, that vision became our reality.

You see, when grace starts to lift for something, you have to start asking yourself a few hard questions. The grace to be on staff at the local church we were a part of had been lifting for the previous five years. Lots of changes were happening and people were repositioning. We knew there was more for us outside of the local church model of vocational ministry, but we couldn't quite see how to get there. God was shifting things and shaking things up for us. He didn't want us to get too comfortable so that when it was time for us to move, we would be ready. We knew God was opening doors in the business world for both of us, but we didn't have clarity – we just had willing hearts. We took a deep, prayerful look at our lives and asked ourselves a few challenging questions about what was working and what wasn't working at the time.

What wasn't working was living paycheck to paycheck. We budgeted fun things into our lives intentionally and spent quality time as a couple and with our kids, however, we weren't quite living at the level of financial freedom we wanted to be at. So, Keith and I started an adventure into a world that was completely foreign to us. We took a journey into entrepreneurship, business, marketing and sales. This journey would become much more than a good idea; it became the new framework to bring us tangible change. I had no idea what this world was all about, but I was intrigued, and wanted to learn more.

A TIME OF
Reflection

Are there any areas you feel the grace is starting to lift in your life?

What areas in your life are working? Which are not working?

What are some things you can begin doing now that will help you transition into your next season successfully?

"Burn the Ships"

_____

_____

_____

_____

_____

_____

_____

_____

DECLARATIONS

I have what it takes to live powerfully and effectively.

I make good choices and wise decisions

I am integrous and trustworthy in my interactions with others.

WE KNEW GOD WAS
OPENING DOORS IN THE
BUSINESS WORLD FOR
BOTH OF US, BUT WE
DIDN'T HAVE CLARITY —
WE JUST HAD WILLING
HEARTS.

I TRULY BELIEVE GOD WANTS
US TO ENJOY THE LIFE HE HAS
GIVEN US, THE BIG THINGS,
THE LITTLE THINGS AND
EVERYTHING IN BETWEEN.

99

Hanging Onto Hope 16

WAS IT SCARY JUMPING INTO A WORLD we knew very little about? Yes, absolutely. However, God has been right in the middle, leading us every step of the way. Every chapter in this book, every story I've shared, there's always been a yes in our hearts to do whatever He wanted us to do. When God calls you to something, He can get you the tools and resources needed to equip you. You just have to say yes and be willing to go on the journey with Him.

The favor has always been there in Kingdom and business spheres for both my husband and me. We just couldn't see it until the timing was right and God revealed it to us. Even though I knew it was God's plan for us, transitioning to Southern California wasn't easy for me. I had a hard time letting go of what was and what could have been. One of the hardest things to let go of was our home. It was a miracle house for us in that season, and we had just started remodeling it. I knew we would have to sell it eventually, and the idea of that was really difficult.

I ran across a picture of Jesus and a little girl online one day that really stood out to me. In the picture, Jesus was holding a giant teddy bear behind His back with one hand while reaching out His other hand to the little girl saying, "Trust Me," but the little girl was holding her small teddy bear tightly behind her back not wanting to give it up. Our house was the same. God was asking me to give up my precious house and to trust Him that He had something even better for us in the next season. My heart wanted to believe, but my mind was getting in the way.

The area we were moving to was going to be much more expensive to live in, but I've walked with God long enough to know that when He calls you somewhere He will provide. Still, unbelief and doubt were trying really hard to rob me in that moment of transition. I had a dream a few months after we moved that our house would sell right around Christmas time, and it did. God kept giving me hope along the way. I love the definition of HOPE: the joyful expectation of good things coming your way. That's the key right there... *HOPE.*

HOPE: the joyful expectation of good things coming your way.

A year later, when we were looking to buy a home in Southern California, things weren't looking very hopeful. We had promises and knew God would open something up, but it wasn't the right time. We looked at so many homes and applied for at least twelve, but when it was time, the right one opened up for us. Then, the Lord reminded me of that picture of Jesus and the little girl. He had something even better than we could have dreamed or imagined. But it required TRUST.

Why do we all dream about things we'd like to step into? Because we have hope for a better or brighter future. We all have dreams, plans, goals and so many different ideas at times.

I know all my life I have been a dreamer. Daydreamer, visionary, call it what you may, but my mind tends to come up with a million ideas a minute. Sometimes I have a hard time communicating just one thought because there are so many. But I find that if a thought roams around in my mind for more than a few days, I'll usually write it down and begin to pray into it. But many times, a thought will come and go after a few hours, so there are certain things I follow through with and others I don't. After many attempts and failures at trying something new and it not working out, I realized that every random thought running through my head is not mine to develop into some great and glorious plan. Sure, we all need to dream, wish and hope for things, but at the same time it's important to be true to and appreciate your present reality. It can be extremely overwhelming at times when you are wired this way, but hang on...there is hope.

We are all in different seasons of life; what worked for us ten years ago or even last year will not work for us now. Life runs its course and seasons change. Have you ever considered that all of your ideas are not meant for you to develop or accomplish? Maybe they are there for you to help someone else get a blueprint for a dream in their heart. Maybe it's your role to help bring clarity and wisdom to a vision they have been carrying in their own heart and encourage them along in their personal journey.

I am finally starting to see the difference. It's taken me several years, and I still get many ideas, but now I realize they are not all for me and I am finally ok with that. I also realize that people like myself can get so caught up in dreaming about what they want to do and accomplish next, that they forget to embrace the season they currently live in. Many times, your current reality represents the fulfillment of dreams that you were praying and believing for in a previous season. If I can encourage you in any way with dreaming, learn to embrace the wonder and joy of living out the dreams of your past. Don't rush and get too busy dreaming up the next big thing and miss your opportunity to live fully present, especially if you have kids. The time with them will pass so quickly that you'll wonder what happened. They will be grown before you know it.

> *Don't rush and get too busy dreaming up the next big thing.*

I truly believe God wants us to enjoy the life He has given us, the big things, the little things and everything in between. I've also heard it said that whoever has the most hope has the most influence. I pray that would be true for you. As you delight yourself in God, He will truly give you the desires of your heart.

Blessings on your journey to finding freedom.

Much Grace,

—Heather

"

We all need to dream, wish
and hope for things, but at
the same time it's important
to be true to and appreciate
your present reality.

"

A TIME OF
Reflection

What have you been dreaming about? Write down as many dreams as you can.

Out of your list, which dreams stand out to you the most? Ask God what He thinks about that and write it down.

Which areas of your life do you naturally have favor in?

"The Blessing"

....

....

....

....

....

....

....

....

....

DECLARATIONS

I have supernatural grace to enjoy every season I am in.

I have hope because God is with me and He is good.

Living in freedom is my birthright as a child of God.

Favor follows me wherever I go.

WHEN GOD CALLS YOU
TO SOMETHING, HE CAN
GET YOU THE TOOLS AND
RESOURCES NEEDED TO
EQUIP YOU. YOU JUST
HAVE TO SAY YES AND BE
WILLING TO GO ON THE
JOURNEY WITH HIM.

99

"Freedom"

Printed in Great Britain
by Amazon